INTRODUCTION

So you've decided to adopt a dog. How

exciting! What kind?

The cute kind? Wait, all puppies are cute! But *will* you choose a puppy, or maybe an adolescent dog, or an adult? Will your new dog be big, medium, small, or, with a mixed-breed puppy, a bit of a surprise? Long hair, short hair, curly hair, wiry hair, no hair? Protective, or a social butterfly? Funny and goofy, or serious-natured? Very active, moderately active, a couch potato?

Hold on a moment, I hear you say. For what reason do I need to respond to this multitude of inquiries? It's simply a canine! For what reason would I be able to simply go out and get a canine, any canine? A canine is a canine is a canine, right?

Well, really...

Every canine is unique. And not just in size, or fur, or the shape of their ears. Each canine is appropriate for an alternate proprietor. The best canine for me may not be the best canine for you, and neither of our canines may be the ideal pet for somebody else.

Let's glance at an example.

Family A's two youngsters, ages four and six, had been bugging their folks for a little dog for quite a long time. Their folks didn't actually need a canine however felt that it very well may be really great for showing the kids liability. On Christmas morning, the guardians gave the kids a wiggly lab blend puppy they had gotten from an asylum the other day. There had just been one youthful doggy at the safe house, so albeit the guardians had expected something little and calm, they hesitantly took what was available.

The youngsters were excited from the get go. Then the puppy started jumping on them and licking their faces while they were trying to open their other presents. The more they pushed the pup down, the more he bounced back up. Whenever he wasn't bouncing on them, he was investigating, biting on wrapping paper and presents, and petty on the carpet.

Finally, the puppy was closed into the restroom, where he woofed and scratched the entryway constant for fifteen minutes. He should be eager, the guardians thought, and passed on the Christmas morning celebrations to take care of the little dog. Whenever they opened the entryway they saw that paint was scratched off it and that there was crap spread all around the floor, none of it remotely close to the paper they had laid out.

They took the doggy to the kitchen and keeping in mind that they were emptying his food into his bowl, he doddled once more. He ate his food, and afterward crapped on the kitchen floor.

By this time the little dog smelled of crap and the youngsters ran shouting from the stinky puppy. He merrily pursued them all around the house, leaving crap paw prints all around the floor covering. Whenever he got up to speed to the four-year-old, he hopped on her back and wrecked her. As she shouted and cried, the guardians saved the doggy back into the washroom. The following day, they returned the doggy to the shelter.

Two days after the fact Family B showed up at the haven. They wanted to take on a pup when they actually had a couple of long periods of get-away to assist him with getting comfortable. They were a functioning family with two pre-teenager youngsters and needed a puppy who could grow up to climb and camp with them. Their exploration demonstrated that a lab or lab blend would be a decent decision. They had examined the haven Thanksgiving get-away however didn't track down a decent competitor. This time they saw the little dog that Family A had returned.

They took the lab pup to the asylum's Get-Acquainted room and went through 30 minutes getting to know him. He was high-energy, yet their quiet conduct quieted him too. They overlooked his bouncing up until he quit hopping, petting him just when he remained down on the ground. Before long he wasn't hopping up by any means. He adored lying on his back on the girl's lap as she delicately scratched his chest. They had brought a few treats along, and observed that this brilliant individual could be effectively directed to sit or rests for a treat. With the preparation to zero in on, he turned out to be consistent and responsive. They concluded this was an ideal little guy for themselves and embraced him.

When the family returned home, the youngsters watched the doggy in their yard while their folks prepared the puppy's region for him. The little guy did his business,
and the kids played a game where they got back to him and forward, hunkering down so he didn't hop up, and remunerating him with a cuddly scratch-fest each time he showed up. Whenever their folks called them inside, they conveyed the little guy to the kitchen, which had been gated off. A weighty water bowl and about six toys of various types were set up on the

floor.

The little guy euphorically started to cavort, play, and bite. Since he was extremely youthful and his day had been invigorating as of now, he started to dial back after around ten minutes of play. Since the children and their father were in the kitchen watching him, they saw when the pup's energy dropped. They took him back outside, where he promptly doddled. Back in the kitchen, the little guy conveyed a bite toy to a delicate towel and set down to bite. In the span of two minutes he was sound asleep.

The family named their little dog Clark, after Clark Kent, in light of the fact that in spite of the fact that he appeared as though a conventional lab blend, they realized he planned to grow up to be a superdog.

Clark the lab pup was a fiasco for Family A, and the ideal pup for Family B. Similar canine, two totally various results. Why?

I'll give you a clue: it had nothing to do with Clark himself.

The effective reception of a little dog (or any age canine) starts with you. Little dogs are not clean canvases. There are superb young doggies out there for practically all people and families. But as we see in the case of Family A and Family B, the same puppy isn't right for everyone.

This book will situate you to be Family B - to track down the right little dog, or canine, that will turn into a cherished piece of your family.

First, we will take a gander at all that should be considered before you choose to embrace a pup or another grown-up canine. What did Family A foul up? What did Family B do right? How might you, as well, be effective from the very beginning?

Next, we will take a gander at the method involved with picking a doggy or canine. How do you have any idea what sort of doggy will be appropriate for you? How would you pick the best
individual for you from a litter? What's more, is it conceivable that you should consider taking on a juvenile or grown-up canine instead?

Finally, we will consider every one of the manners in which you could obtain your doggy, from the promising to the possibly disastrous.

Most individuals go through hours investigating another sleeping pad, days exploring another vehicle, and weeks, months, even years investigating another home or new position. The time you spend observing the right thing or circumstance is indispensable, on the grounds that it will be essential for your life long into the future. However practically nobody spends in excess of a couple of moments adequately long to look into the location of the closest pet shop or asylum exploring the right canine ally for the following ten-to-fifteen years of their life. So like family A, they get a canine, any canine, and generally they don't keep it.

Every canine (other than the youthful pups) that you find in a haven is there since it was somebody's off-base choice.

This doesn't need to occur. I don't need it to happen to any canine or any proprietor. I don't need it to happen to you. Every one of those canines is as yet the best decision for somebody. One of them may be ideal for you. If not, we can find the canine who is.

This book will assist coordinate you with your Dream Dog, a canine that will be a delight for you from the day it shows up in your home until the finish of its life. It contains all that I've learned in over thirty years of working with canines and proprietors: the most and most disastrous motivations to get a canine; how to sort out what sort of canine is best for you; how to observe that fantasy canine and bring it home. Since most of proprietors start with a doggy (and pups require the most work), a large part of the book centers just around pups, yet the last segment takes similar standards and applies them to getting a juvenile or grown-up dog.

I've seen many families effectively embrace and structure lifetime bonds with astonishing canines by following the practices in these pages. You, as well, can observe the canine of your fantasies, one who is and will remain actually, intellectually, and sincerely steady, and one who will constantly be "the best canine of all time" until the finish of its days.

Let's prepare you for your Dream Dog!

PART 1:

Getting Ready For Your Dream Dog

Do you REALLY want a puppy?

"obviously I do!" you might think. "I'm perusing this book, aren't I?" And you might be correct. Yet, inquiring as to whether you need a doggy isn't like inquiring as to whether you need another TV. It's significantly more complicated.

For a certain something, youthful pups are basically the same as creeping children. Both find out about the world by investigating everything in reach and by placing things in their mouths. Neither shows up house prepared or ready to convey. Neither comprehends "proper" conduct, and both will commit a ton of errors as they learn it. Both need consistent management and care during the earliest phases of their lives. Both require monetary result, time, and consideration from you-regardless of whether you want to give it. And neither will grow up to be a calm, relaxed adult without thoughtful guidance from you while they're young.

Here are a few accommodating inquiries you can pose to yourself to decide whether you
truly need a puppy:

- Are you willing to decide on the best type of puppy for you and your lifestyle, and then wait for that puppy, if necessary?
- Can you resist cute puppies that are not likely to grow into the right kind of dog for you until the right one does come along?
- Every puppy will need a great deal of your time and attention for the first six to twelve weeks of its life with you, even when you are tired, busy, sick, or don't feel like it. It will continue to need daily time, attention, supervision, and guidance until it is approximately 18 months old. How much time and energy do you have to give a puppy? Are you ready to make that degree of commitment?
- Do you understand and accept everything that is part of a normal puppy's behavior? Are your expectations of a young puppy realistic? Will you educate yourself about kind, humane ways to modify or redirect those behaviors so that they mostly occur when and where you want them to? (Hint: the Resources list in the back of this book can help!)
- If you want a dog for your children, do you also want one for yourself?

Keep your solutions to these inquiries as a top priority as we come. Perceive how you feel before the finish of the book.

Here's another inquiry: for what reason do you need a puppy?

Do you want a furry friend to cuddle with? A guard for your home? A playmate for your kids? A cute "child" that you can be parent to without totally giving up your life? An exercise partner? A responsibility lesson for an older child? A companion to grow with you?

Some of those reasons are extraordinary. Some of them are not. In the following part, we'll take a gander at a few normal reasons individuals get doggies or embrace canines according to the little dog's point of view as well as our own-and perceive how a few reasons are obviously superior to others.

Why I (Think I) Want a Puppy!

There are bunches of various reasons individuals need a pup. How about we take a gander at a few of these reasons and consider whether we figure they will bring about a cheerful result for individuals and pup.

Reason 1: So the puppy can grow up with the kids

Young youngsters and pups appear to be a mysterious mix. Television is continually showing us ads where cheerful youngsters run in a field with a pup at their heels, infants and pups are nestling, or children and canines are getting into delightful wickedness together.

But assuming that the camera ran somewhat longer, we could get to see an alternate side to kids and pups: the one where the snuggling doggy begins biting on the child's fingers and the child begins to shout; where the little dog makes up for lost time to the running kids and hops on them, thumping them to the ground; where a drained and harried parent with no capacity to bear naughtiness, but charming, yells at the kid and the pup, sending the kid to his room and unloading the pup outside.

Puppies and small kids can have brilliant minutes together, on the off chance that they are painstakingly checked. But puppies, like toddlers, want to be in motion every waking moment. And for baby dogs, that means exploring the environment, including human skin, with their teeth. It implies running and jumping,
digging and biting, pulling and snarling, until they breakdown into sleep.

Few guardians of little youngsters at any point say "I wish I had one more small kid to deal with!" Yet for the main months of a pup's existence with its family, the family fundamentally has another baby. Little dogs should be administered each waking second, and when you likewise have a youngster who fits that depiction, you have quite recently got serious about your occupation as a parent. Recall what occurred in doggy Clark's first home, with Family A? That wasn't an exaggeration.
That's actually the thing happens to ill-equipped families who take on a pup while they have youthful children.

Would you be ready to really focus on an extra little youngster for a little while? On the off chance that not, think earnestly before you get a puppy.

Reason 2: For my (older) child who desperately wants her own puppy

What about a youngster mature enough to really focus on a little dog herself? The mindful adolescent young lady or kid who doesn't have anything on their birthday list aside from a puppy?

This can work, yet provided that the guardians know that regardless of how much the kid yearns and asks for a doggy, no kid ought to at any point be relied upon to be exclusively answerable for the lifetime of the dog.

An offspring of ten or eleven isn't fit for understanding making a twelve-to seventeen-year obligation to a social creature who needs day to day connection to remain solid and happy.

First of all, does the kid need the canine however much she needs the pup? A pup just stays nearly nothing and charming for a little while prior to transforming into a lanky juvenile and afterward a grown-up canine. Assuming the kid is enamored with young doggies, getting one will just fulfill her for the exceptionally brief time frame before the little dog starts to develop up.

Secondly, a kid will not actually comprehend the stuff to deal with a doggy they've never gotten it done. Saying "you truly do acknowledge it will be your occupation to

take this doggy outside at whatever point it necessities to go, to hold it back from biting things up, to go for it for strolls and to pup classes, to prepare it to be an extraordinary canine… " is unreasonable. Obviously any kid who needs a little dog will gesture energetically and demand that she will do that large number of things - yet she has no casing of reference for what that will really mean. She will probably put forth a valiant effort, however you, the parent, will be the person who should get a move on if and when it slips she's mind or doesn't follow through.

Thirdly, pups and youthful canines need consistent management. Who will really focus on the little dog then-canine while the youngster proprietor is at school, doing schoolwork, at sleepovers, away at camp, or going to after-school and end of the week sports practice and occasions? That amounts to a great deal of hours when another person will have to take care of, activity, train, and play with the youngster's little dog/dog.

And finally, whatever you longed for when you were eleven, was that the same thing you continued to wish for with all your heart when you were thirteen? Sixteen? Nineteen? A young dog that was desperately wanted as a puppy may find itself upstaged by a growing child's social life, extracurricular activities, dates, etc. Yet the dog still has the same daily needs for attention and care. The average lifespan of a dog is 12-15 years. That eleven-year-old child will be off to work or college, possibly in another town, possibly even starting a family of his own by the time that puppy grows old.

If your more established kid loses interest, are you prepared to step in to raise, care for, and love the dog?

Reason 3: My wonderful dog was

important to me growing up, and I want my children to have that experience too.

This can be fine. But keep in mind that 1) your children are not you, and 2) it's unlikely that you were the person actually raising that childhood puppy you remember. Your folks, and perhaps more seasoned kin, did a ton of that work for you-you were simply excessively youthful to notice.

Be certain your youngsters really need a family canine. They may not be essentially as intrigued as you, or they may be too occupied to even consider partaking in the new little dog more than occasionally.

And that great canine you recollect from your youth? Somebody went to the difficulty to raise and prepare a pup so it turned into that superb canine. For this situation, that individual will be you. Do you have the extra time and energy in your life for this project? And the knowledge to do it properly? High hopes and happy memories are not what it takes to create a great family dog. It takes instruction, a lot of time and work, and loads of patience.

Reason 4: I need to get more exercise. If I have a dog, I'll walk it every day and get healthier.

Getting a doggy in the expectations that it will drive you to be more dynamic is unreasonable for the canine and ridiculous for the vast majority. To practice with another canine, have a go at fostering another strolling plan on your own first. Perceive how lengthy you keep it up, and the amount you appreciate it. Certain individuals really do observe they appreciate new work-out schedules, yet a lot more battle to keep up with them and return to their old, inactive ways of behaving rapidly. A canine won't make you need to practice on the off chance that you would as of now prefer not to-you might even come to loathe a high-energy canine that should be strolled all the time.

A canine isn't a treadmill. You can't simply involve it for some time, conclude you don't want to utilize it all things considered, and transfer it to the cellar. A canine is a living being with everyday necessities that should be met, whether or not it is addressing your requirements or not.

Be mindful: a pup won't be an appropriate distance strolling or running accomplice until it is developed. Little dogs can experience genuine, extremely durable harm to their bodies assuming they are made to over-practice while they are as yet developing. As a general rule, a canine should be about a year old before it begins practicing with you, contingent upon the person. It's fundamental to have a veterinarian check your canine for actual adequacy before you do any lively activity with him; if

he has any muscular issues like hip, elbow, or shoulder dysplasia, exercise can aggravate those issues. What's more, consistently develop your canine's activity gradually and progressively, similarly as a human would have to do.

It's difficult to track down a decent canine strolling or running accomplice. Some canine varieties are inadmissible for running by any stretch of the imagination, others experience issues breathing whenever strolled excessively far or excessively quick, and many have strides different enough from the human walk or run that moving at our speed is troublesome or excruciating. We'll speak more about which breeds are great activity accomplices when we talk about picking the right canine for you.

Finally, training a dog to walk or run comfortably with a person while ignoring oncoming people and other dogs generally requires the help of a competent professional and a long learning period before both owner and dog are happy and comfortable. And although a dog may eventually learn to walk or run alongside a person, that is not a dog's preferred way of "taking a walk." Dogs need to pause and sniff intriguing spots. Be certain your canine accomplice gets some wander and-sniff time alongside the exercise.

Reason 5: I really want a puppy, I know I have the time and energy to raise one, and I am eager to learn what I need to know to choose one wisely, so that the puppy joining my home will grow into a dog I will keep and love all its life.

This is awesome, and I could even say the main, motivation to get a pup. You really want to truly need a canine, since that canine will require a lot of your consideration and take up a lot of your time (a little dog substantially more than a grown-up canine, yet all canines need time and attention).

According to Seattle Purebred Dog Rescue, the #1 explanation proprietors surrender their pets isn't a conduct issue. It's "no time for the canine." Examine your life

now, truly, and be sensible. Do have the opportunity to raise a doggy into an extraordinary dog?

And it's so critical to pick the right pup or canine. Any canine coach will let you know that some alleged "conduct issues" are brought about by a confound among proprietor and canine. "My canine necessities more activity than I can give it." (Then for what reason did you pick a youthful Labrador Retriever blend?) "My canine pulls like insane on strolls." (A Siberian Husky blend wasn't the most ideal decision to abstain from pulling.) "My canines battle constantly." (Getting female terrier littermates made this a possible result.) The right canines for those proprietors were out there, yet the proprietors didn't have the information they expected to settle on the most ideal decisions for them as well as their canines. They procured their canines incautiously, without speaking with specialists, doing research, or getting ready for success.

So you've analyzed your explanations behind needing a pup and concluded they are the right ones. That's a great start! But having your heart in the right place isn't all that's needed. In the next chapter, we'll look at everything— absolutely everything—you'll need to have, do, be, and know to be a great puppy and dog owner.

Do You Have What It Takes To Be A Great Dog Owner?

So presently you realize a doggy is presumably ideal for you. But are you right for a puppy? That's not as easy as it sounds. Just needing the little dog, regardless of how certain you are that you truly do need it, isn't to the point of ensuring that you'll have a decent encounter and a cheerful, sound canine. There's significantly more required to have been really prepared to turn into an effective canine owner.

To prevail with regards to raising a doggy into a great canine, you will require the accompanying:

1. Time

Your new canine will require a lot of your time, particularly in the event that you get a youthful doggy. In its initial not many months with you, you will in a real sense should know about where your doggy is and what he is doing each snapshot of the day. Keep in mind, a 8-week-old doggy is comparative in numerous ways to a creeping child without a diaper on. Could you leave that child solo? Amazingly, numerous proprietors do precisely that with their young pups, and afterward feel irate and shocked to observe things bit and mishaps on the floor covering. Young puppies, just like crawling babies, need supervision 100% of the time, unless they are resting in a safe and secure confined space such as a crate or an exercise pen (the equivalents of a crib and playpen for a baby).

The requirement for extremely extraordinary management goes on for the initial a few months that a pup spends in its new home. Also, the developing youthful canine will keep on requiring oversight when individuals are home and repression when

they are not until he is around year and a half old. Indeed, that appears to be seemingly forever. But young dogs left unsupervised too soon develop habits such as furniture-chewing, repetitive barking, and counter-surfing. Canines who don't have those valuable open doors when they are youthful sometimes if at any time foster those propensities during their grown-up lives.

Another important way your puppy will need your time, from his arrival in your home to the age of about 16 weeks, is for socialization outings. A puppy needs to be socialized so it gets used to the world. This socialization period is crucial to the puppy's development, as it determines how the puppy views what is safe vs. what is scary for the rest of its life. The pup must be carefully exposed to all the things it will be expected to react to calmly during the rest of its life. You, the owner, must take the puppy out into the world almost every day during those weeks, and orchestrate the outings so that they are positive events for the puppy. The goal of socialization is for your puppy to build good associations with riding in a car, meeting strangers, being around children, passing by other dogs calmly, hearing the hiss of buses and the wail of sirens, feeling grass and gravel and wood chips under his feet, smelling city smells and country smells, and so much more. This must happen at this stage in your puppy's life no matter what season you get him in, something to consider if you have brutally hot summers or frigid winters.

There is no real way to overemphasize how significant this socialization period is. A pup who spends this whole period in somebody's patio won't ever be loose and open to taking strolls or cooperating commonly with outsiders. He won't ever take new encounters in his step. He is probably not going to be protected with youngsters or outsiders, albeit that may not be evident until he develops. The lamentable truth is that a doggy who isn't as expected associated before the age of 16-18 weeks may not at any point be a decent family pet.

Do have opportunity and willpower to appropriately mingle a little dog for the initial two months he is living with you, and to regulate him cautiously for the first year?

2. Money

Whether you purchase an expensive thoroughbred or embrace a "free" pup starting from the family

the road, pet possession isn't modest. Puppies need a series of vaccinations in their early months in order to be protected against common diseases, then occasional vaccinations throughout their adult lives. Great quality little dog food helps the pup foster well actually and can forestall issues like persistent looseness of the bowels or skin sensitivities that colors and fillers in modest food sources can cause. Cartons, child entryways, practice pens, chains, collars, ID labels, micro processors, bowls, toys, treats - these are on the whole fundamental things a little dog needs and the costs add up. Most will require fix/fix a medical procedure eventually. And of course, accidents happen, so be prepared to pay emergency veterinary bills. You will not spend very as much on a doggy as on a human youngster yet it could appear to be that way sometimes.

3. Energy

Can you stay aware of a youthful pup? During puppyhood and a large portion of a canine's first year, conscious = progressing, running and hopping and playing constant until they nod off once more. And they will not be able to sleep through the night for the first few weeks, so you will need to find the energy to have your sleep interrupted once or twice (or more) to take the puppy outdoors.

4. Knowledge

Humans don't naturally have the foggiest idea how to construct incredible associations with canines. A considerable lot of us have never watched any other person effectively raise a little dog. Regardless of whether we had a pup as a kid, we may not recollect what it took to raise it from pup to canine. This absence of information can harm what could somehow be a superb connection among proprietor and dog.

Most individuals counsel specialists while making significant buys and ventures. Oddly, not very many individuals do this while picking a sidekick canine to be essential for their family for 10 years or more. Research lets us know that most forthcoming pup purchasers counsel nobody prior to buying a pup; not so much as a veterinarian, a pet inventory store worker, or a neighbor with a canine, not to mention a genuine expert.

Family A's pup purchasing experience was a calamity and a disappointment. Why? Since they figured they would sort out some way to deal with a little dog on the fly. They went out and incautiously took on the most readily accessible little dog, which turned out to be an unfortunate decision for their family, and brought it home having obtained no information about how to raise it and having made no arrangements for its arrival.

Many individuals invested substantially more effort, thought, and investigation into picking a vehicle, a house, a school for their youngsters, a shared asset, an insurance contract, even a sleeping cushion than they do a puppy.

Fortunately we live during a time where experimentally legitimate and accommodating data is promptly accessible. It's not hard to figure out how to do the right things, particularly once you know how to filter through the deception and track down the great stuff. The asset list at the rear of this book can assist you with doing that. But you have to actually do the research and acquire the knowledge before your puppy arrives. What you don't know can and will hurt both you and your pup to-be.

5. Patience

It might shock some first-time canine proprietors, however young doggies are not conceived getting human language. They get familiar with the importance of words the same way human children do: by quiet reiteration, matching word with object or action.

No one surges infants with regards to learning language. But people seem to think that puppies are born understanding the word "no" and will respond to every other word they are told after hearing it just once or twice. *Nothing you really do can cause a little dog to learn quicker than its normal improvement permits it to.*
As with a child or baby, you should be ready to go through months persistently showing your doggy all that you need it to know, and comprehend that there will be numerous stumbles en route. Being ready to confront even the most disappointing slip-ups with affection and tolerance is a significant piece of being prepared for a puppy.

6. Everyone else in your family on board with you

Unless you're single and live alone, you're not the one in particular who will interface with this little dog consistently. Does everybody in your family need a doggy? Is everybody able to be patient and reliable with treatment, jargon, and preparing? Pups are a consistent, dynamic presence in a family. It is ridiculous for the pup to bring it into a home where somebody doesn't need it, or where somebody will attack the cautious raising and preparing being finished by the remainder of the family. So assuming that you live with others, talk honestly together about these issues.

Here are a few inquiries to consider with your family, flat mates, as well as live-in partner:

- Have everyone's preferences been taken into account so that the new arrival can be as close as possible to the whole family's dream
- dog? Who will be the main caretaker for the puppy? That person needs to be enthusiastically on board in order for this to be successful.
- If there are children in the family, what role will they play in caring for the puppy? Are the adults willing to step in when the children are busy or lose interest?
- Are there regular visitors, such as elderly relatives, dog-allergic individuals, or families with babies or toddlers, that you need to consider? What about the neighbors? It's your puppy, but if they're anti-dog, it could be a problem.
- Does your family have other pets? How will you bring a puppy into their space and ensure harmony?

Whew! OK, I know that is a great deal to contemplate and examine. But if you consider carefully and decide that you do have all six of these areas covered, then chances are excellent that you can adopt and raise a happy, well-adjusted puppy.

Now we should zoom out and take a more extensive perspective on groundwork for a pup. There are a few things that all canines and little dogs will do. Few out of every odd canine will do
each activity, however pups will do the vast majority of them, so be prepared for them all.

Normal Behaviors of Puppies and Dogs

For all their numerous distinctions, all canines share a great deal practically speaking. Here are a few ways of behaving that you will see with pretty much every dog:

- Barking
- Growling
- Chewing
- Biting
- Digging
- Running
- Jumping
- Urinating and defecating
- Vomiting
- Helping themselves to any food they can reach (aka "counter-surfing")
- Rolling on the ground
- Walking through mud
- Shaking themselves off when wet, wherever they happen to be
- Chasing anything moving fast

Many dogs will also do some or all of the following:

- Howling
- Fixating on a caged bird, hamster, or other small pet
- Chasing small animals and killing them if they can catch them
- Shredding paper and other
- objects Disemboweling soft toys
- Eating poop and vomit
- Rolling in smelly dead
  things

The things in these rundowns are essentially typical canine characteristics. They are essential for the bundle marked "Canine," similarly as talking, cleaning out our noses, expecting to utilize the latrine a few times consistently, strolling upstanding, and chuckling are important for the bundle named "Human."

How might you feel assuming somebody attempted to prevent you from doing any of those ordinary human ways of behaving? However proprietors frequently express a wish to "prevent the canine from yapping" or "prevent the canine from biting things" and soon. Ordinary ways of behaving ought not be closed down, however they can be made due. Your responsibility is to help your pup or canine when and where to play out every one of those ways of behaving, and to deal with the climate so conduct you don't need can't occur. For instance, in the event that you don't need your canine to destroy delicate toys, give him tear-safe toys without stuffing, hard elastic toys, as well as other safe options in contrast to "stuffies." You can likewise stay away from ways of behaving you don't need via preparing substitute ways of behaving. A canine who is lying on a mat in the kitchen can't be counter-surfing for goodies.

Remember, it will be your responsibility to regulate or accommodatingly keep your puppy at whatever point he is conscious until he is sufficiently adult and taught to the point of settling on the right decisions and act fittingly. As I referenced before, you should show your doggy benevolent and persistently, as you would a slithering child. *Continuously recollect that what is ordinary way of behaving for canines isn't, as a rule, typical way of behaving for us, and bad habit versa.*

Sadly, many individuals raise their little dogs utilizing a lot more extreme strategies than they could at any point use with their infants. Rather than tending to botches with persistence, benevolence, and delicate instructing, numerous proprietors rebuff their young doggies, as though some way or another these child creatures showed up in the house knowing the contrast among good and bad, and decided to foul up on purpose.

The little dog in the present circumstance has no clue about why he is being rebuffed, just that he has left the glow and security of his mom and littermates to land where his ordinary doggy ways of behaving might be met with encouragement,
might be overlooked, or may cause discipline. One model is bouncing up on a proprietor's leg, something little dogs normally do. At times hopping might be supported (proprietor thinks pup is adorable and snuggles it). Now and again it gets overlooked (proprietor is on the telephone and dismisses). And sometimes it is punished (owner is wearing dress clothes and kicks the puppy away).

Not just does this confound the doggy, it likewise startles him, since he can't be sure whether he may be rebuffed for doing something that works out easily for him. And if punishment continues, the puppy is likely to become defensive and may snap or bite. It is extremely hard for affection and devotion to fill in an environment of discipline and dread. How might you feel about functioning for a manager who appeared to generally be searching because of motivations to rebuff you? What about one whose relationship with you resembled a coach's, in light of direction and praise?

Why do as such many individuals holler at and smack their little dogs? Since, to be honest, it is significantly more straightforward than taking the time and energy important to direct them through puppyhood generous and insightfully. Additionally, discipline is remunerating to the punisher. It alleviates our annoyance to yell or smack. The pup flees, looking blameworthy, and we have the extra help of reasoning "I despised doing that, yet it did the job."

But the truth of the matter is that the main thing the discipline genuinely refined was to make your pup start to fear you. What has all the earmarks of being a look of responsibility on a canine's face is really a look of pacification, saying "kindly don't holler at/hurt me any longer." A canine who is shouted at or smacked for doing a typical canine way of behaving fail to see the reason why that happened anything else than you would comprehend somebody strolling up and smacking you for wheezing, brushing your hair, or doing some other ordinary human behavior.

If a way of behaving was done in some unacceptable spot or at some unacceptable time - a mishap on the mat, the TV remote being bitten, your kid's shoe gladly conveyed in from his room - the doggy isn't the person who committed an error. Your doggy or canine is letting you know he isn't far enough along in his turn of events or his figuring out how to settle on the ideal decisions yet. To assist him with learning the ideal decisions in a steady climate, a pup or a canine new to a family should generally be in one of the accompanying three situations:

- Actively supervised by a responsible person, indoors or out
- Actively engaged, learning correct behaviors through play
- Humanely confined in a crate, exercise pen, or safe room behind a baby gate.

Would you start a work project on your PC with a slithering child unaided in the house? Obviously not. Leaving a doggy or undeveloped youthful canine, or any canine new to a family, free in the house can bring about mishaps, bite blemishes on seat legs, and even injury to the canine from biting an electrical line or gulping Legos. So while you're administering this new doggy, you're not simply preparing and mingling it. You're additionally ensuring it stays safe.

To complete out this segment, how about we investigate what that management resembles by inspecting day to day existence with a youthful puppy.

A Day In The Life

Puppies, such as creeping children, are minimal relentless investigating machines. Extremely youthful doggies (under roughly 12 weeks) can't be anticipated to stay asleep from sundown to sunset without something like one potty break, frequently more right away. A normal 24 hours with a 8-week-old little dog for the most part looks something like this:

12am: Take crying pup out of his carton and convey him outside to potty, then, at that point, return him to his case. Endeavor to sleep.

4am: Repeat.

6-7am: Take whining puppy outside to potty, then to the kitchen to feed him breakfast. He eats, drinks, then must go outside to potty again. Sit on the floor and play with puppy for 10-15 minutes, then outside to potty again. Pup bites on toys in the gated kitchen while you set up your own morning meal. Following 10-15 minutes, pup searches for a spot to rest. You tenderly move doggy to carton at 8:30am. He complains briefly and afterward settles.

10:30am: Puppy wakes and cries. You take pup outside to potty. Pup approaches water (constantly when in the kitchen play region). Puppy drinks, then plays for about ten minutes and begins to circle. You rapidly take pup outside and he potties. You play outside with the little dog, he at last potties once more. You bring him inside, he bites on toys and plays.

12pm: You allow him his second feast of the day. He eats, drinks, and necessities to go outside to potty. Once back inside, he plays momentarily and afterward searches for a spot to rest. You put him into his case at 12:45pm.

3pm: Puppy wakes and whimpers; you take him outside to potty. You put the doggy in his box in the vehicle and drive to your kids' school. You sit on a seat close to the jungle gym with the pup on your lap for fifteen minutes so he can see and hear the movement without being excessively close (this is an incredible illustration of organized socialization). Kids who need to pet him are welcome to offer him one of the treats you brought along, on a level hand, while giving him three delicate strokes with the other hand.

3:30pm: You and your kids return home from school. After the pup potties in the front yard, the kids play with the little dog in the kitchen, sitting on the floor, extravagant toys in their grasp for pup to bite on, generally under your cautious management. You give pup a potty open door around at regular intervals, observing cautiously to see when he begins to sniff the floor or circle.

4:30pm: You leave little dog in the gated kitchen, having splashed the counters at his biting level with hostile to biting shower like Bitter Apple and provided him with a few enticing bite toys. You mean to set the kids up with their schoolwork, yet you get occupied and don't get back to the kitchen for 30 minutes. Pup has had a mishap. One of the youngsters takes him outside while you tidy it up completely with an enzymatic cleaning arrangement like Nature's Miracle. Pup returns inside, having pottied again outside.

5pm: Puppy gets his third dinner of the day, beverages, and afterward goes out for another potty break. He is worn out and goes into his box all alone to rest. You unobtrusively hook the door.

8pm: Puppy wakes and cries in his container. You take him outside to potty. You take a portion of his toys to the front room to sit on the floor and play with him during a TV show, with one eye on the show and one eye on the doggy. He comes to the third promotion break (around 45 minutes) and you understand you're going overboard, so you take him outside, where he promptly potties. Back inside, he plays quietly on the floor with you for another twenty minutes or so, then curls up in your lap to sleep.

10pm: You convey him outside for a last potty of the evening, then, at that point, put him into his carton close to your bed. He whines for a brief time frame and afterward falls asleep.

Next day: Repeat, supplanting the little dog's socialization excursion with an alternate one.

Remember how long a youthful pup will require from you? That was no misrepresentation. An average day for a little dog is in a real sense a 24-hour day, and you'll be available to work for pretty much every last bit of it. But as you can see, a regular routine can be developed when you're home with the puppy through the day. You could finish some work while the pup's napping.

But what might be said about when everybody is away from the house during the day? Assuming you're single and go to work, or the two guardians in a family work outside the home, your doggy should spend a significant part of the day home alone. This isn't great. Pups are social child creatures, so it is difficult for a youthful little guy to invest such a lot of energy alone.

Your doggy will require a feast in the day until he is roughly four months old (pups change in how lengthy they need this third dinner; their lessening revenue in it shows that they might be exchanged over to two suppers per day). So somebody should stop by around noon to take care of the puppy.

A puppy can manage a work day alone in a long-term confinement area such as an exercise pen or a secure and puppy-proofed room as long as he gets his midday meal. His space needs to contain an arrangement of safe bite toys, towels in a carton with the entryway eliminated for security or a bite safe bed to rest in, water in a weighty bowl or cut to the side of the pen so it can't be toppled, and a thick layer of papers totally covering the floor. Assuming you are worried about the floor, place a canvas under the layers of paper. Hope to have numerous mishaps to tidy up when you return home and conceivably a little dog to wash. And remember that it is still vital that the pup gets out regularly for socialization before he reaches 16 weeks of age.

A superior option is to observe somebody able to come in to take care of and play with the doggy for some time eventually during the day. A neighbor could be
enchanted. There are proficient canine sitters who can play out this errand also. You could even observe somebody who might be excited to have you

drop off your little dog each stir morning and get him again in the early evening. The pup would have the advantage of an alternate house, various individuals, and various encounters, the doggy sitter would have a pup to appreciate for half a month, and you would have a lot more joyful and better mingled little dog.

Pups grow up rapidly, despite the fact that those initial not many weeks can feel timeless. Rest periods develop longer yet there are less of them. The little dog's capacity to control his bladder and guts improves progressively. At last he will begin staying asleep for the entire evening in his case. It will be numerous months yet before he can securely meander the house unaided, yet the requirement for every minute of every day consideration will drop away. Life will begin to appear to be typical once more; a new "ordinary," with a doggy in it.

CONCLUSION

Ready For
Rover

So by this point, you should know significantly more obviously assuming you're prepared to embrace and raise a pup. We should review:

- You feel that your reasons for wanting a puppy at this point in your life are good ones.
- You are willing to educate yourself about the best ways to raise a puppy or introduce a new dog to your household before you get
- one. You have enough time to supervise and socialize a puppy for its first 2-3 months with you.
- You have the money, energy, knowledge, and patience to support and love a new puppy.
- Your family and anyone else who will interact with the puppy are excited and ready.
- You're familiar with the things all puppies and dogs do, and you're prepared to meet them all with patience and kindness.

- You can set up a puppy care daily schedule that works well for you and the puppy.
- You've been reading everything covered in this section and thinking "yes, yes, yes, yes, yes!"
- *Or,* you may be less sure that a puppy is right for you but excited about the prospect of finding the right adolescent or adult dog.

If these things are valid, you're prepared to find and pick your fantasy

canine! However, which canine will that be?

The following segment of this book will assist you with addressing that inquiry. How about we take a

take a gander at all the great assortment in the realm of dogs.

PART 2:
Choosing Your
Dream Dog

A Dog Is Not A Dog Is Not A Dog

What kind of dog will be the best pet for you? Even with all the preparation and consideration from Part 1, bringing the wrong dog into your home may well create an uncomfortable, frustrating situation for both you and the puppy. So before you can pick the doggy that will turn into your ideal canine, you should invest in some opportunity to consider which of the many sorts of canines you truly care about. How would you envision your "fantasy canine"? How can it look? How can it behave?

Although many individuals perusing this book are contemplating observing the right doggy, let us generally remember that you will just have a pup for a couple of months, trailed by numerous years with a grown-up canine. All young doggies are cute and attractive. But they grow into dogs with very different needs, looks, and personalities.

So how about we quit thinking "little dog" for a couple of seconds here and think about what sort of canine you need to live with for the following ten years or two. There are a wide range of canines, from the minuscule Maltese to the gigantic Leonburger, from the slim Whippet to the bulky American Staffordshire Terrier, from the profoundly dynamic Australian Kelpie to the smooth Clumber Spaniel.

One of the most helpful spots to begin is with what the variety or blend of breeds you are keen on was initially reproduced to do. It's anything but a happenstance, for example, that Labrador Retrievers act uniquely in contrast to English Mastiffs. The Labrador Retriever was intended to recover birds out of water after the birds had been shot by trackers. To this end, Labs have the elevated degree of energy required for running in the field the entire day, a medium-minimized body size, and a water-repellent coat. Most have an energy for conveying things in their mouths, are obsessed with swimming, are mindful of their proprietors (as need might have arisen to be to their trackers), and wouldn't fret doing dull errands - they could have been expected to recover many birds in a day's chase. While there are exemptions, most Labs are by and large cordial and nice, not fit to monitor canine duty.

English Mastiffs, then again, were reared essentially as property guards. They need work out, yet under a canine reproduced to run in the field with a tracker day in and day out. Since they were not expected to work under the course of a human yet expected to monitor a bequest all alone, proprietors could need to work somewhat more diligently to get and keep their consideration. Their incredible size accompanies a few disadvantages; they have a more limited future than little or medium measured canines, and the doggies should be managed cautiously to stay away from injury as they develop into their huge bodies. English Mastiffs can be dubious of outsiders except if all around associated to them as pups, and are normal watchman dogs.

What about blended breed canines? Blended breeds are only that, a blend of breeds. Most have some recognizable variety attributes. It is significant to consider Labrador Retriever qualities while considering taking on a blend that resembles a Labrador Retriever. The equivalent goes for other blended breeds. But since every mixed breed dog is an individual and different from all the others, sometimes no foundation breeds can be identified. In these cases, assess the canine on a singular premise. We'll address how to do this little further along in this book.

In the following not many sections, we will take a gander at a few elements to consider as you think about what kind of canine would be best for you.

5

Energy level

Energy level is quite possibly the main element to think about while searching for the right canine. You may be excited by seeing a line collie jumping up high after a Frisbee, or enchanted by an English Bulldog napping before a chimney. Both are extraordinary canines and can be ideal pets for the right proprietors. But if a border collie is right for you, an English Bulldog will not be, and vice versa. This is the place where it is vital to genuinely consider your regular life.

A line collie is one of the greatest energy breeds on the planet. Envision the energy level expected to remain in charge of a moving group of sheep the entire day, consistently. Line collies likewise need the elevated degree of insight important to expect each move made by a group of erratic creatures, and to have the option to counter those moves in a flash. Taking on a boundary collie is a not kidding responsibility of time and energy. Giving a boundary collie hardly anything to do baffles the canine's regular drive to go through its days being occupied and useful. This dissatisfaction brings about "issue ways of behaving", which can incorporate biting furniture to pieces or biting through dividers, wild hyperactive way of behaving or potentially woofing, or hysterical dislodged "crowding" conduct like pursuing kids and gnawing their heels or pursuing bicycles or vehicles. A confined border collie with no way to occupy its busy mind and body may eventually turn to self-mutilation behaviors such as chewing the skin off the backs of its own paws.

If you need an accomplice for high-energy canine execution exercises, or grouping, or to prepare in an assortment of ways of aiding you around the house and yard consistently, a boundary collie may be for you. Assuming you're a relaxed individual who anticipates calm strolls and delicate play with your canine, or who is out of the house most days and not around to connect consistently with your canine, a collie is
doubtlessly not the canine for you.

At the opposite finish of the range, the English Bulldog is an extremely low-energy breed, which has likewise been reared with such a distorted gag region that it can't inhale regularly. Strolling a bulldog when it is over 70F outside can in a real sense kill the canine from heat surrender. Running and dynamic play with such a canine is impossible. This would be an appalling variety for an imminent proprietor searching for a climbing friend or a contest nimbleness canine. But bulldogs are generally easy-going and can be a fine choice for a
low-energy family who appreciates calm time at home - particularly on the off chance that they don't care about some wheezing and slobber!

There is a wide range of energy and activity levels in dogs of all sizes. Papillons and Miniature Pinschers are dynamic yet tiny; English cocker spaniels are dynamic and medium-sized; Rhodesian Ridgebacks are dynamic and huge. Newfoundlands are exceptionally huge canines with a low movement level; Basset Hounds are low-energy and medium estimated; Pekingese are little, less dynamic dogs.

While we're discussing energy level, we likewise need to discuss strolling (and running) with your canine. Most canines have a characteristic step that is too quick to ever be agreeable for individuals to stroll alongside. Numerous proprietors resort to putting a squeeze or gag choker on their canines to make them stay ready, regardless of how awkward that is for the canines. Envision being compelled to stroll at a speed that isn't normal for you for significant distances consistently, with torment as the result of attempting to dial back or accelerate. Assuming piece of your new canine's life will be going with you on strolls or runs, pick a sort of canine with a fitting energy level - and be ready to draw in a decent mentor to help both of you become genuine accomplices when you are making the rounds. Preparing a canine to walk or run serenely with an individual while additionally overlooking approaching individuals and different canines by and large needs the support of an able expert and a learning period.

There are some breeds well suited for long steady running, such as Dalmatians, German Shorthaired or Wire-haired Pointers, Weimaraners, and northern sledding breeds such as Siberian or Alaskan huskies. These canines, or blends of them, are worth thought assuming you need a running accomplice, and assuming you are sure that you will really run routinely. These varieties can't be

transformed into habitually lazy people in the event that you conclude that the dynamic life isn't so much for you. All canines who are expected as running accomplices need a vet check to ensure they are actually steady enough for running, and afterward a program of molding that forms time and distance slowly.

Some dogs shouldn't be walked at all, or only very carefully. Toy canines ought to never be utilized as exercise-strolling or running accomplices; regardless of the amount they appear to run around at home, it is awful to compel their little legs to stay aware of yours out on an activity walk. Keep in mind, with a chain on, they have no real way to stop assuming the walk turns out to be a lot for them. "Brachycephalic" dogs (those with pushed-in faces, such as English bulldogs, French bulldogs, Boston terriers, and more) cannot be walked in warm weather nor should they ever be forced to walk long distances because they cannot breathe properly under those conditions. Monster breeds can walk all around ok yet are unsatisfactory for running. A few different varieties, like Basset Hounds and Dachshunds, are additionally inadmissible for significant distance strolling or running. This is a point to investigate prior to picking the right kind of canine for you, on the off chance that this is one of your significant issues.

So ensure you give your own energy level and exercise routine a decent hard look, and afterward research which sorts of canines are a solid match. Your canine will thank you for giving it a perfectly measured proportion of activity!

Attachment

When you envision investing energy with your canine very still, is that canine in your lap, on the floor alongside your seat, or across the room biting a toy? Does it wait regardless, get up when you do, intermittently approach have its ears scratched, or sit under you, gazing into your face, hanging tight for you to accomplish something interesting?

In other words, how much do you want to interact with your dog when you aren't walking or playing with it? And how much physical contact do you want? Different types of dogs have very different levels of desire for physical contact.

Do you need a shadow wherever you go? Or on the other hand could you incline toward a cheerful canine with a periodic pat and kind word? A few varieties, like Chow Chows, Basenjis, and Akitas, are now and again portrayed as "standoffish." This doesn't mean they are threatening or don't bond with their proprietors, simply that they probably won't require similar measure of direct cooperation or petting consistently as a few different kinds of dogs.

Other breeds are nicknamed "velcro dogs," because they prefer to be near, even touching, their owners *all the time*. Numerous Doberman Pinschers, Bernese Mountain Dogs, and Golden Retrievers are in this gathering. And many dogs are in between these two extremes, enjoying being stroked but also happy chewing a toy while lying near you.

As with energy level, want to be petted and snuggled doesn't continuously coordinate with the canine's size. Little terriers are occupied little creatures, reproduced to be always

keeping watch for vermin to chase and kill, and may not appreciate nestling for broadened timeframes. Then there are Irish Wolfhounds who will attempt to settle their 150 pounds onto your lap if you sit on the floor and give them the opportunity!

Think about the fact that it is so vital to you to have a canine who is generally glad to be stroked or held. Might it annoy you to have a canine who was continuously sitting and inclining intensely against you at each open door? Then again, could your sentiments could be harmed if your canine once in a while (or never) needed to nestle with you? Assuming a specific degree of love is critical to you, ensure you pick a kind of canine who will cherish giving it to you-and will gobble it up when you return the favor.

7

Protectio
n

Is essential for this canine's occupation going to be to make you aware of expected risk? Or then again even to shield you from conceivable harm?

Guard canines fall into two classifications - alert canines, whose yelping can drive away gatecrashers, and genuine assurance canines, who can back up bark with chomp if essential. Even a small alarm dog is a good deterrent to crime; intruders want to break into a house in stealth and silence. Most hunting canines, like dogs, retrievers, setters, and spaniels, are not normal insurance canines, but rather they can be fantastic caution canines. As a matter of fact, essentially all canines will sound the alert on the off chance that they see or listen to something of the normal, except if they have been rebuffed for doing as such. This is normal and requires no training.

Dogs known for their defensive inclinations incorporate German Shepherds, Rhodesian Ridgebacks, Belgian Malinois, and breeds created to monitor or group runs, like Great Pyrenees, Kuvasz, or Australian Cattle Dogs. Usually assurance isn't the just or even essentially the essential capacity of breeds like these, however they truly do perform watch/security conduct normally. Concerning tiny canines, there have been a few situations where gnawing Chihuahuas have ruined assaults on their proprietors. So size doesn't continuously matter!

There are two significant admonitions about security dogs.

First, while nothing bad can really be said about needing a canine who can safeguard you, that can't be the main motivation to get a canine. These canines need a similar consideration and association with you as some other canine, consistently. Lying around your home hanging tight for a potential gatecrasher won't be enough for them. In the event that you obtain a genuine assurance canine, be ready to prepare and mingle him

from puppyhood, continue socializing throughout the dog's lifetime, and possibly participate in activities such as schutzhund (a protection-related dog sport), agility, and K9 nose work to keep your smart dog mentally occupied.

These dogs tend to be medium to large, strong in body and will, and will need regular physical as well as mental exercise. They are best for experienced proprietors who get the requirements of their variety, and who have the opportunity and energy to give them what they need to remain actually and intellectually healthy.
Please recall that any canine can give a powerful alert. Try not to feel that you want to get a gatekeeper breed assuming all you truly need is a canine who will bark assuming that somebody goes onto your property.

Second, canines normally safeguard their region (house, yard, vehicle) and individuals they are clung to. They needn't bother with "security preparing" to become viable alert or assurance canines. Certain individuals have the mixed up impression that the most ideal way to make a security canine is to segregate it from outsiders, or to treat it generally. These are not the ways of making a powerful gatekeeper canine. Those are the ways of making a hazardous dog.Dogs with a characteristic watchman nature should be mingled completely to outsiders as young doggies. They need to have many great encounters with individuals they don't have any idea, so they get that individuals, *as a rule, are not a threat.*
Otherwise such a canine is a stacked firearm that could go off anyplace - similarly prone to go after a meeting companion or a pizza conveyance individual as an intruder.

This socialization won't make your canine an insufficient alert or insurance canine. Entrust your canine's bond with you. He will know when somebody is a danger to you, *except if you have instructed him that everybody is a danger, or separated him so everybody is odd and frightening to him.* Kindly don't make a perilous dog.

Sociability

If you are normally a timid individual, do you figure somebody could drive you to outgo? Assuming you are social and well disposed with everybody, what might it take to make you modest and resigning? We realize that individuals are brought into the world with individual characters. These person qualities are a blend of what we acquire hereditarily from our folks, how we are raised, and what encounters we have as we develop up.

Dogs have individual character contrasts, as well. While a doggy's character is affected by its mom and kin, and by its encounters during its first long stretches of life, there are additionally permanently set up contrasts in little dog characters similarly as there are in people. Every individual doggy in each and every litter is not quite the same as its kin, similarly as human kin are regularly altogether different regardless of having similar qualities and the equivalent parents.

Some canines answer in a cordial way to everybody, all individuals, all canines. Some adoration all individuals yet just like a couple of canines they know well. Others are careful about certain sorts of individuals, like youngsters. A few canines are not happy around some other canines. Part of the way this is an element of the dispositions of the parent canines, mostly the way in which well the canine was associated during its puppyhood; likewise, a horrible mishap could lifelongly affect canines' sentiments about individuals or different canines. A canine of mine was hopped on during puppyhood by a benevolent yet wild English Bull Terrier; my canine responded with guarded hostility toward each and every other Bull Terrier he saw all through his life. But there are also breed tendencies toward friendliness or reserve.

Learning which demeanor characteristics you are bound to find in specific types of canines, or in blends of those varieties, will work on your possibilities getting a canine whose degree of amiability is the thing you are looking for.

Do you need an active canine who loves everyone, coexists well with most different canines, and is only a charmer overall? Your most obvious opportunity for this sort of disposition is to take a gander at breeds that were reproduced to work with individuals and with, or in closeness to, different canines. Hunting canines - retrievers, setters, spaniels, pointers, and furthermore many dogs - and scaled down renditions of these, like King Charles Spaniels, are regularly amicable with basically everybody. Northern spitz-type breeds such as Keeshonds and Siberian Huskies are also often relaxed with other people and dogs.

Are you interested in a dog who will bond strongly with your family but won't really be interested in buddying up to strangers? Dogs whose protective instincts have been enhanced through breeding are less often immediately accepting of everyone they meet. This includes personal protection dogs such as Giant Schnauzers and Bullmastiffs, property and flock guards such as Tibetan Mastiffs, Schipperkes, and Rottweilers, and herding dogs such as Australian Shepherds and Bouvier de Flandres.

The ubiquity of canine parks can persuade individuals to think that all canines love the organization of different canines. That is valid for certain canines, however numerous others feel in an unexpected way. Terriers, too as a few different varieties, can be spunky with different canines. A few kinds of canines are basically centered around their family and don't have any desire to communicate with different canines. A few more established, noble canines don't need doggies or young adult canines in their space. Canines who were taken from their moms too early or were ineffectively associated as little guys can show improper canine non-verbal communication, which can befuddle different canines and make tense situations.

Talk with specialists about how the sort of canine you are thinking about by and large answers different canines. And if you are adopting an adolescent or adult dog from an unknown background, do not subject that dog to daycare, dog parks, or other situations where it will be forced to deal with dogs it does not know. When you realize your new canine better, you can cautiously attempt a few acquaintances with different canines, preferably with the direction of a certified proficient trainer.

Remember that as well as the propensities of breeds and types, person socialization has a major effect in how canines feel about different canines and about individuals. An inadequately mingled retriever is probably going to be less agreeable than an all around mingled mastiff. So if it's important to you that the puppy you acquire will be generally friendly, first look for a puppy in a naturally social breed or type, then follow puppy socialization guidelines very carefully.

Grooming Needs, Shedding, and Allergies

The last factor to consider has nothing to do with a dog's personality, and everything to do with its fur coat! And it's one important reason to think about the dog your puppy will become, rather than the puppy it may be now. Barely any youthful little dogs need any preparing past nail trims and brushing. This makes it simple to fail to remember that the sweetheart Poodle doggy, for example, will require proficient preparing consistently when it is a grown-up canine. So will the Afghan Hound, the Airedale, the Cocker Spaniel, and the Lhasa Apso, among others. The Australian Shepherd who isn't brushed routinely will foster bunches of hair. The excellent white layer of a Samoyed can mat in the event that not prepared routinely, and can abandon white to brown after a frolic in a sloppy yard. Male canines of any variety or blend in with long hair on their stomachs will at times get pee on that hair when they lift their legs.

Keeping canines of certain sorts spotless and very much prepped can be tedious, costly, or both. It could be definitely worth the difficulty for you to have such a wonderful canine... however at that point once more, it may not. And all canines will require some type of preparing, regardless of whether it's simply a fast brush and nail trim each week.

Unless canines practice an incredible arrangement on a harsh surface, they will all require their nails managed consistently. *This isn't discretionary.* Canines whose nails become too lengthy can't walk easily, and in the long run their feet can endure harm. There have even been instances of canines whose nails developed as far as possible around and penetrated the stack of their feet. Many individuals are not happy managing canines' nails themselves, and many canines are bashful about having their feet

dealt with. A decent custodian can tell you the best way to manage nails securely, or grind them with an exceptional processor called a dremel device, which many canines like to managing. In the event that you can't manage your canine's nails, you should have this expertly done on an ordinary timetable, whether your canine requirements other expert preparing or not.

Now, about shedding. Practically all canines shed. Some, like Golden Retrievers and German Shepherds, are famous for leaving floats of hair everywhere.
Short-haired dogs such as Vizslas can shed just as much as long-haired ones, leaving prickly little hairs all over the furniture and the carpet. Welsh Terriers and other wire-covered terriers don't shed, however on the off chance that they are not expertly prepped ("stripped") routinely, their delicate undercoat will turn out to be free to the point of adhering to furniture they possibly look for some way to improve against.

Most canine proprietors acknowledge that living with canine hair is simply aspect of canine possession. But if that thought appalls you, consider the non-shedding breeds: all three sizes of Poodle, the Bichon Frise, the Maltese, and the wire-coated terriers are some examples. But remember, as mentioned before, these dogs have professional grooming requirements that must be fulfilled for them to remain truly non-shedding.

"Labradoodles," "Cockapoos," "Goldendoodles" and different canines whose name closes in "- doodle" or "- crap" are cross reared among Poodles and another variety. Regardless of whether these blended variety canines shed relies upon which parent's "shedding qualities" are prevailing in that specific canine. There can be shedders and non-shedders in a similar litter. Since pups shed very little or not in the slightest degree, *it is basically impossible to tell with these poodle blends until they are grown-ups whether they will shed or not.*

Finally, certain individuals search for non-shedding breeds in view of "canine sensitivities" in the family. Sadly, it is a canine's skin dander and not canine hair that triggers unfavorably susceptible responses. In opposition to what numerous commercials for poodle blends guarantee, *there is no such thing as a hypoallergenic type of canine*. Some canine sensitivity victims are even adversely affected by poodles themselves. Assuming you especially need a canine however you or somebody in your family has canine sensitivities, consider encouraging a canine of the kind you are thinking about, or "getting" a companion's or relative's canine, to check whether the sensitivity victim has a response. It would be terrible for both individual and canine to proceed with a reception of

a canine or doggy just to observe that the victim can't live with the new expansion to the family.

These actual variables may not appear as significant as matching your canine's energy level or amiability to yours, however that doesn't mean you ought to overlook them! Actual properties like prepping needs and shedding, in the event that they aren't big issues themselves, can be extraordinary main consideration between at least two great expected canines. An incredible canine with negligible prepping needs may very well be a preferable fit over a likewise extraordinary canine that should be brushed consistently or expertly prepared each month.

CONCLUSION

Exceptions To The Rules

This segment has recorded numerous instances of various varieties known for various characters and ways of behaving. Invest in some opportunity to explore those models one of them may be actually the canine you're searching for. Assuming none of the models here appear to be very appropriate for you, that is fine as well. There are something else to find out about and browse. Glance through the Resources area toward the finish of the book for more information.

There are special cases for this multitude of breed speculations. There are quiet boundary collies, cuddly Fox Terriers, bashful Brittany Spaniels, and Rottweilers who love everybody. There are canines of all breeds whose mentalities toward people or different canines have been impacted by an absence of socialization, unforgiving preparation, or oppressive treatment. There's no assurance that you'll get precisely the character you want.

But assuming specific characteristics are critical to you, your most obvious opportunity with regards to getting what you need is to get a canine variety or comparative blend known for the characteristics you're searching for. Follow that up by picking the best person for you that you can find. Assist with that is coming straight up in Part 3.

So presently you realize you're prepared for a little dog, and you have a thought of what sort of canine you need that pup to develop into. You're at last all set out and track down that fantasy little dog! Section 3 takes a gander at picking a doggy, thoroughbred or blended breed. Section 4 will address the choice of tracking down the right juvenile or grown-up canine to adopt.

PART 3:
Finding Your Dream Puppy

Once you have concluded what kind of grown-up canine would squeeze a ways into your life, now is the ideal time to ponder observing the right doggy that will develop into that grown-up dog.

The primary thing to comprehend is that each little dog is unique, even inside a similar variety, even inside a similar litter. Contemplate your youngsters, or you and your kin. No two people are the same.

There are two stages associated with tracking down a fantasy pup. The initial step is realizing where to get the right sort of pup in the first place. Then you need to discover how to choose the right individual puppy. This part will walk you through both of those steps.

10

The BEST Place To Find Purebred Puppies

The best hotspot for a thoroughbred pup, without a doubt, is a side interest raiser. A side interest raiser is somebody who produces little dogs for affection for the variety, not for profit.

Hobby reproducers are devoted to delivering a line of genuinely, intellectually, and sincerely sound instances of their variety, where every age enhances the last. They rarely work with multiple varieties, and most frequently only one. They know about clinical issues normal to their breed(s) and perform hereditary testing and wellbeing screenings to guarantee that main really sound and solid people are bred.

Hobby reproducers are exhaustive, merciful, and care profoundly about where their young doggies end up. A leisure activity raiser will need to meet you and your family, talk about the variety with you, and examine your expectations and objectives for your future pet. They will absolutely love to show you their offices and acquaint you with their grown-up canines, who ought to be either open and well disposed or smoothly affable, contingent upon the idea of the variety. Assuming their grown-ups are bashful, growly, or avoided you, come up with your considerate reasons and leave. Stay away from that raiser. He could have dear young doggies, however assuming he conceals his grown-up canines from you, that lets you know that you won't observe your fantasy canine at his facility.

Hobby reproducers could have pet hotels, yet their canines will invest at minimum some energy in the house. Their pups should be brought up in the house, so you get a doggy who is now used to family sights, sounds, and scents, and OK with the comings and goings of people.

A leisure activity raiser may or probably won't acknowledge your application for one of their
pups. Recollect that they are not reproducing to bring in cash. They have a genuine, long haul interest in their rearing system and each doggy they produce is valuable to them. Most leisure activity reproducers will anticipate that you should sign an agreement, in which they will spread out what they expect of you in your consideration of the doggy they have so affectionately raised, and what you might expect of them. A decent leisure activity reproducer's agreement will incorporate an explanation that they will take their pup back anytime in its life would it be a good idea for you at this point not have the option to or need to keep it.

If you are acknowledged, the raiser will remember your expectations and objectives consistently as she watches the doggies from birth, and will offer you the one, or conceivably a decision of two pups, who she thinks will be the best counterpart for you. You could view as the modest female delightful, for instance, yet the reproducer is pondering as long as you can remember with the canine, and knows from her experience that this little dog will continuously be excessively little and sensitive for the dynamic climbing and running life you have laid out as your ideal. Whenever you enjoy picked a side interest raiser, trust her judgment. She has as incredible a stake in the progress of this situation as you do.

Finding a side interest raiser is easy. Most leisure activity reproducers are associated with breed, execution, or game clubs. Instances of breed enlistment associations are the Australian Shepherd Club of America, The United Kennel Club, the American Kennel Club (AKC), and the American Rare Breed Association, all of which keep up with arrangements of reproducers partnered with their groups.

Many raisers sign a Code of Ethics when they join their association. They keep severe guidelines of lead in their rearing practices. Notwithstanding, you genuinely must research your planned breeder(s) to guarantee that you are OK with their practices, from moral contemplations to functional doggy raising. Contact any raiser whose canine varieties you are intrigued in. Start with a discussion, find out about one another, visit face to face or over Skype if possible. Now and then it very well might be feasible to go see canines a specific reproducer has delivered at canine shows. By earlier game plan, you could possibly converse with the reproducer there also - however be certain you really do make earlier courses of action, and don't move toward her until she has completed in the ring.

Hobby raisers don't raise their canines regularly, and their little dogs can be costly. A leisure activity reproducer's rearing project is a vital piece of their lives, not a beneficial business. These reproducers put an extraordinary arrangement in each litter of pups. Costs incorporate top quality nourishment for mother and little guys, inoculations, wellbeing screenings, enhancement for the developing doggies, and considerably more. The expense of your pup covers most or at times those costs. Side interest raisers only sometimes create any gain on their litters. Any cash they really do make returns into the reproducing program.

Hobby raisers typically have just a couple of litters a year probably, and regularly every pup is as of now represented by somebody who has been on the reproducer's hanging tight rundown for quite a while. So don't anticipate bringing back a pup from your first gathering with a leisure activity raiser. Be willing to wait for the right puppy, or for a space on the breeders waiting list to open up.

The pause and cost will be worth the effort. Assuming you observe the right side interest reproducer, you will have deep rooted taught help from her and a solid, sound, appropriately began little dog that will really turn into your fantasy dog.

11

Other Recommended Sources for Puppies

If you are searching for a blended variety pup, or need to investigate various hotspots for a thoroughbred puppy, here are a few choices to consider:

Rescue groups

Most varieties have their own salvage associations. These are controlled by individuals who know and love that specific variety and will commit time and energy to tracking down new homes for undesirable or deserted canines of that variety. There are public, state, local, and neighborhood breed salvages. The most effective way to observe them is to go to a web search tool and enter "salvage" and the name of the variety you are searching for, in addition to any extra data you need to incorporate. Model: "Oregon English Springer Spaniel rescue".

Besides rescues for individual breeds, you can also find rescues for groups of similar breeds, such as rescues for sighthounds or herding breeds. A few regions have umbrella gatherings like Seattle Purebred Dog Rescue, Inc., which handle many types of canines through associations with person "breed delegates" or single-breed salvages. These umbrella gatherings play the agent among you and the variety of canine you need, and can be exceptionally useful in the event that there is certifiably not a specific variety salvage near you. There are likewise salvage bunches who handle doggies and canines by region or area, whether or not they are thoroughbred or blended breed. These can be superb hotspots for puppies.

With any salvage association, be ready to finish up administrative work, to be consulted, to ask and be asked numerous inquiries. Heros treat their stewardship of destitute canines extremely in a serious way These canines have as of now lost one home (or more), and they need to be exceptionally sure that the new home each canine goes into has the most ideal possibility being its ideal and last. There will be an agreement to sign, laying out your obligations to the canine and the association's liabilities to you. You'll likewise have to pay a reception expense or gift for a salvage canine. Most heros are volunteers and their endeavors are upheld generally, now and again totally, by donations.

Will salvages have thoroughbred young doggies? Seldom, on the grounds that most of saved canines are teenagers and grown-ups. But it does happen. Assuming you need a doggy just, make that reasonable front and center and ask how regularly pups come into that association. Obviously there can be no assurance - a salvage gathering could deal with three litters one year and none the following. Breed and locale have an influence in that: a German Shepherd salvage could answer that they in all actuality do get a few pups in consistently, while a Lakeland Terrier salvage could see you they regularly don't get one grown-up canine each year, not to mention a pup. Various pieces of the nation see floods and shortages in various varieties, at various times.

It's additionally useful to be clear about what you mean by "little dog." While I consider that puppyhood closes at 16-18 weeks when canines become youths, many individuals utilize the term significantly more freely to allude to creatures under a year old, in some cases much more seasoned relying upon when that specific variety develops. Assuming you need a little dog between 8-12 weeks old enough, you really want to say that.

Thoroughly look at any salvage you intend to work with. They range from fantastic to horrifying in their practices. Anybody can gather creatures and call herself a salvage association. Even a well-meaning or widely recognized rescue group, when inundated with puppies and dogs, can lose sight of the importance of making the right match. Search for an expertly worked and all around run bunch, with a spotless office or encourage homes, with canines who look sound and answer well to you, undeniably associated with a variety club or some other parent association. Look into references and check them.

Vet offices and hospitals

Another hotspot for doggies is your veterinarian or creature clinic. Clients regularly contact their veterinarians for help observing great new homes for pets they can't keep. Assuming you make your veterinarian mindful of what you are searching for, the person can guide proprietors of likely possibilities to you on the off chance that any happen. The greater part of these will be grown-up canines, however here and there a relative ends up being oversensitive to another doggy, or benevolent grown-up youngsters give a little dog to an old parent who doesn't need or need a youthful pup in her life.

Neighbors/farm dogs/yard signs/flyers

When I was a kid during the 1960s, nearly everybody I knew got their canines thusly. Fixing and fixing was not normal and canines regularly ran the neighborhoods with their kids, so litters happened reasonably frequently. These days it is interesting to stumble into a litter of doggies playing in somebody's yard, as a result of the progress of the development to fix and fix pet canines. But occasionally a friend's or neighbor's dog has a litter, or a "puppies for sale" sign can still be seen on a drive in the country. Certain individuals set up fliers on local area announcement sheets in places of worship, eateries, or bistros promoting accessible little dogs from a "shock" litter.

These "unplanned" pups need cautious assessment, yet many can become incredible pets. On the off chance that the mother and father both have great cordial dispositions, the mother is very actually liked during her pregnancy and keeping in mind that she is nursing, assuming the young doggies are brought underneath up in the house where they experience the sights, sounds, and scents of regular day to day existence and get affectionately dealt with, they might well end up being fine pet dogs.

But take care that you don't trade your fantasy pup for the most helpful doggy. It tends to be difficult to say no when a neighbor, companion, or relative is trusting you will take one of their young doggies. But if the litter parents are big, active dogs and your dream is to have a cuddly lap warmer, proceed with caution. Continuously recollect you are settling on a decision for the following 15 years of your life, not only for the couple of long stretches of puppyhood. Pick the pup that will develop into the grown-up canine you really want.

Animal shelters

Shelters could get young doggies frequently, or very sometimes. It relies upon the region where the sanctuary's creatures come from. Protects seldom get thoroughbred pups. At the point when they do, they are quite often either an undesirable gift or the "extras" from an unexpected or terrace breeding.

You're significantly more prone to track down blended breed pups in covers than thoroughbreds. Be that as it may, with the exceptionally viable fix/fix program in the United States, many safe houses don't get blended breed young doggies regularly. Converse with your neighborhood covers, let them know what you are searching for, and ask how frequently they would anticipate such a pup in their office. A few havens have holding up records and will get in touch with you in the event that a doggy or canine of a kind you are searching for comes in. With most, however, you should continue strolling through and checking regularly.

With these choices, make sure to remember your rules for what you need solidly. All doggies are charming, yet you are searching for your fantasy dog.

12

Puppy Sources to Avoid

The sources in the last two parts are altogether great spots to search for another little dog. However, I additionally need to educate you regarding two places never to search for one: pup factories and pet shops.

So-called "little dog plants," or business reproducers, are something contrary to side interest raisers. They produce pups for one explanation as it were: to bring in cash. And in order to make the greatest amount of profit, they breed as many dogs as possible and spend as little money and effort as possible on those dogs.

The grown-up canines in pup plants are taken care of modest food, kept in uncovered, foul enclosures, and compelled to raise each opportunity a female becomes game. They are not prepped, not worked out, given at least clinical consideration, and took care of just when essential. All grown-up canines fit for rearing are reproduced, whether or not they are cripplingly timid, forceful, or experience the ill effects of ailments that they can give to their puppies.

Pup plant little dogs get none of the dealing with and mingling so imperative to ordinary pup improvement. They are auctions off as youthful as could be expected. They show up at their objections as charming as some other little dogs, however they are ticking delayed bombs of clinical and demeanor issues prone to come.

So, a pup plant climate is a painful life for its grown-up reproducing canines and the absolute worst beginning for doggies. Doggy factories flood the market with perilous, unsocialized, undesirable, and unready pups, not many of which will at any point be great pets. *Try not to purchase from them.* Disparaging doggy plants is supporting creature mercilessness and exploitative, and getting a little dog from that climate will be a horrendous encounter both for yourself and for the dog.

Pet shops have been the customary objective of pup plant pups for numerous years. Notwithstanding what the general population might hear, *any doggy you find in a pet shop came from a pup plant.* Mindful leisure activity reproducers actually interview each expected proprietor of one of their pups, to guarantee that each painstakingly raised little guy gets set into the home where both proprietor and canine are probably going to be glad all through their lives. Pet shops have no such assessment process, either for proprietors or canines, so leisure activity reproducers stay away from them-however pup factory proprietors love them, for precisely the same explanation. *Kindly stay away from pet shop young doggies at all expense.* The least demanding way is to just never enter a pet shop that sells puppies.

How can you say whether you're taking a gander at a pup factory little dog? As the general population has become more instructed about staying away from little dog processes, these money crop reproducers have become all the more shrewd and sharp about staying away from simple ID. You could experience them available to be purchased straightforwardly from the rearing office, or through pet shops, or recorded on the web or in paper promotions. They frequently to go incredible lengths to have all the earmarks of being only a customary family with a litter, to attempt to trick the general population into purchasing pups from them.

Here are ways of being certain you don't unintentionally purchase a little dog factory puppy:

1. If the "raiser" doesn't meet with you however is basically ready to take your cash and give you a puppy.
2. If the "reproducer" will not permit you to visit his office ("home") - as a rule offering the "comfort" of meeting you some place to trade cash for puppy.
3. If you can't meet the mother of the litter.
4. If a promotion or site records multiple varieties accessible, particularly - yet not dependably - little varieties (there are a not very many great leisure activity raisers who produce more than two breeds.)
5. If the list includes mixed breeds disguised as purebreds, with made-

up names combining the breeds in the mix, such as cavipoo, chitese, yorkidoodle, etc. (I have no objection to mixed breeds, but an ad listing several breeds that includes these indicates a puppy mill that is trying to cash in on the fad for "designer dogs.")

6. If a web-based ad shows individual pups with costs connected (in any event, showing individual little dogs without any costs joined is a warning; side interest raisers don't need expected purchasers to come see a

   litter with their heart previously set on a specific pup that probably won't be the right one for them.)

7. If a reproducer assumes your installment by means of acknowledgment card online.

If any of these is valid, you have more likely than not exposed a pup mill.

You might feel as though you need to "save" one of these pups. Please think again. Purchasing from doggy plants adds to the hopeless, sad existences of the parent canines and the development of little dogs as though they were sequential construction system items with next to no quality control. Owners who have succumbed to these feelings of compassion have reported incidents such as losing a five- month-old Golden Retriever to crippling hip dysplasia, spending thousands of dollars on skin conditions that cannot be cured, experiencing aggressive biting in a twelve-week-old puppy, and more. It's not worth it.

Ensuring that your doggy had an extraordinary beginning to existence with a blissful and sound mother, great essential consideration, and adoring socialization with people is the ideal way to existence with a fantasy canine. Ensure you search for yours in places that can and will affirm they work thusly and no place else.

13

How do I choose my dream puppy?

Once you've observed a decent hotspot for your pup, the following issue is picking the pup itself.

If you are purchasing a little guy from a side interest raiser, trust her to direct you in choosing the best doggy for you. Recollect that she has been watching, really focusing on, and dealing with these doggies ordinarily each and every day since the snapshot of their introduction to the world, while you have just seen the litter sometimes, perhaps once. And as a hobby breeder, she has as great a stake in the success of her puppy placements as you have in finding your perfect puppy. Each little dog she puts conveys her "pet hotel name" and addresses the sort of canine she delivers to the public.

As a rule, utilize the information on any individual who has been watching and really focusing on a litter of pups you are keen on. Many experienced salvage people and encourage homes can assist you with picking a little dog whose personality they feel will be the best fit for you.

But at times you will be offered a decision between at least two pups. Or on the other hand, assuming you get your little guy from an asylum, a companion's or alternately neighbor's litter, a salvage litter, or another comparative source, you could have to choose your doggy without a reproducer's or pup raiser's direction. How would you assess the distinctions between individual puppies?

One of the absolute most effective ways to begin assessing a litter of pups is to collaborate with their mom. Truth be told, this is vital to such an extent that assuming the mother is in the home or office however you are not permitted to meet her, that more likely than not implies there's an issue the raiser doesn't need you to see. On the off chance that that occurs, leave and there. Try not to purchase from a let raiser you meet the mother of the litter.

The mother has a gigantic measure of impact over how her young doggies end up. She not just contributes half of their qualities, she sets the model for them of how a canine ought to act. In research, typical doggies put with a timid mother canine as babies become bashful themselves as they developed. *So in the event that you try to avoid the mother canine, on the off chance that you don't feel you would be extremely cheerful assuming your doggy wound up like her, don't bring back home one of her puppies.*

Once you've met the mother (in the event that conceivable in asylums and salvages it may not be), you can begin meeting the pups. Assuming you can, visit when the little dogs have stirred from a rest, eaten a dinner, and are prepared to play. Do the little dogs look solid, excited, and occupied? Assuming that the litter looks undesirable, search somewhere else for your fantasy canine. Try not to envision that a condition like a skin rash, the runs, retching, or torpidity will fundamentally clear up once you get a doggy home. Some won't ever do. There are not many things however unfortunate as gaining a cute little dog who may be sick, and watching it get consistently more diseased and ultimately die.

If the litter overall appears all good yet there is one doggy who is exceptionally peaceful, stays in a corner, and additionally dismisses the wide range of various pups' endeavors to play with it, don't pick that pup. At worst, it may be ill, but even at best, that is not the normal cheerful temperament that we want to see in healthy puppies.
Don't be enticed into thinking this is only a "tranquil" little dog that will develop into a "peaceful" canine. Genuinely and typically sound pups are dynamic during playtime.

To get to know the various young doggies, sit on the floor in the pup gathering and watch every one of the cooperations. Request the raiser for some from the young doggies' toys. Continuously have one in your grasp, and proposition it to bombastic little dogs so they won't bite on your skin. Stroke with one hand while the puppy is locked in with the toy in your other hand. Remain until the little dogs are slowing down and searching for spots to twist up and sleep.

Remember that young doggies, during play, practice every one of the abilities they would require assuming they planned to grow up without the consideration of people. The intuition to practice all aspects of the tail pursue kill prey cycle is available in all little dogs, whether they are Alaskan Malamutes or Pekingese. Typical ways of behaving that you are probably going to see include:

- Puppies playing, sometimes very roughly, with barking and the occasional yelp.
- Lots of running and chasing.
- Tug games with toys, with growling
- Shaking soft toys violently (to "kill" them).
- Tearing toys apart.
- Chewing on each
- other. Mounting each other.
- Biting each other.
- Stopping play suddenly to get a drink, to urinate, or to poop.

Observe which young doggies approach you and which don't. Look for human attachment behavior, such as a pup bringing a toy onto your lap and settling down to chew it, or lying against your hip, however briefly. A doggy who is as of now leaned to search out the organization of people can possibly turn into an incredible pet canine. A doggy who shows next to zero interest might turn into a fine pet, as well, yet getting and keeping this little guy's consideration might be even more a test rather than the person who offers consideration freely.

As the pups begin to dial back only a tad, delicately get every pup and perceive how they respond to being held. It's typical for them to be a piece squirmy. But which puppies look up at your face? Be sure you are smiling and your eyes are soft so you don't intimidate them.

You can likewise get up and stroll around a little (mix, so as not to step on anybody). Which puppies are intrigued, and follow you? Which look yet don't follow?

By the time the little dogs begin to tire and settle down to rest, you will have begun to consider every one to be a person, with its own character. While the boldest little guy might have pleased you, or the shyest puppy might have enchanted you, the human connection ways of behaving are your best piece of information with respect to which pup is probably going to turn into your fantasy dog.

So we should audit. To assess and pick the perfect individual pup, you are looking for:

1. A mother canine you love, assuming you are sufficiently fortunate to meet her
2. A little dog who is friendly and fun loving, obviously sound and happy
3. A doggy who is open to being handled
4. A pup who effectively draws in with you, in any event, for exceptionally brief times of time

All pups are delightful. But it's very possible that none of the cute puppies in a particular litter will seem "just right" to you. Feel free to say "much appreciated, yet no way." There will be different litters to check out, and you will know when the little dog of your fantasies shows up. Try not to think twice about something that will be so vital to your life for 10 years or longer. Choose the doggy that will turn into your fantasy dog.

One keep going idea on picking a little dog. As you watched the litter play, did it begin to turn out to be clear why it's such a test to raise a youthful little dog? A considerable lot of the ways of behaving of pups that are typical for them are risky for their people. Doggies put their teeth on everything, similarly as youthful human children at a specific stage set all that they get into their mouths. That isn't an issue when they have hard cleaned littermates to bite on, however when you bring a little dog home everything from the edge of the Oriental floor covering to the TV ropes to fragile human skin is a potential bite object. This need to chomp and bite can't be "remedied": it truly is a need while a doggy is youthful. Whenever the doggy grows out of that stage, it will come by itself with practically no requirement for adjustment assuming it has been taken care of well during that stage.

An eight-week-old little dog needs to eat three times each day, drink quite often, pee up to 17 times each day, and crap somewhere around four times each day, regularly more. It requires some investment and exertion, persistence, and consistency to help a youthful doggy through its infancy and while heading to turning into your fantasy canine. Fortunately assuming that you set forth this energy and exertion, on the off chance that you stay patient and reliable, when your pup turns into a juvenile at 16-18 weeks old enough, you will have set the most ideal starting point for your fantasy canine's future. But if watching the energy and activity of the puppies made you think twice about bringing such a demanding young creature home, there is another great option.

PART 4:
The Adult Dog Option

So, imagine a scenario in which you have perused this book and, considering your life cautiously, you have understood that a pup might be utterly horrible for you right now-yet that you couldn't want anything more than to take on a grown-up dog?

That's incredible! A grown-up or a juvenile canine can be a fantastic option in contrast to a doggy. A large number of similar contemplations apply likewise with a pup; it's vital to pick the right canine that is ideal for yourself as well as your family. But adopting an adult dog can be much easier than getting a puppy. In addition to the fact that numerous grown-up canines previously associated with are essential house habits, there are something else to pick from.

In the present chaotic world, numerous proprietors who begin with good motives figure out that they are too occupied to even think about offering a canine the time and consideration it needs and merits. But those owners' loss can be your gain—as well as your new adult dog's.

14

Pros and cons of adult vs. puppy

When you take a gander at a pup, you can tell in the vaguest of terms what sort of canine it will develop into. As we've seen, getting a specific variety and purchasing or embracing from a respectable source can build the possibilities of your new pup developing into the fantasy canine you need, however there are no certifications. There is a lot more prominent level of "what you see is what you get" with a canine who is as of now grown.

This is especially evident when you can notice the canine in a home climate, either its own unique home or a cultivate home. Canines don't flourish in cover conditions. A few canines shut down, others are continually disturbed, hopping and yelping. Some gatekeeper type canines, with no domain or individuals of their own in a safe house to watch, might actually give off an impression of being more nice than they will be the point at which their new region is laid out and they have fortified with their new individuals - and consequently have something to monitor once more. Converse with the safe house staff about any canine you are keen on, and invest however much energy as could reasonably be expected in a "get-familiar" region with the canine. Consider: on the off chance that the canine never different from what you are seeing today, could you need it? Never embrace any canine expecting it will change, *or that you can transform it*. It could change. But it might not.

Many grown-up canines show up at their new homes house-prepared and with great house habits. All typical grown-up canines have far more noteworthy bladder and entrail control than any youthful doggy, so they will just have to go external a few times each day rather than much of the time. Most completely grown-up canines won't be the habitual chewers that young doggies and most juvenile canines are, either-however all canines ought to approach satisfactory bite toys at all times.

Some grown-up canines as of now walk pleasantly on chain, and may definitely know how to answer a few normal prompts, for example, "sit" and "down." Adult canines have

grown-up minds and grown-up abilities to focus, and with the right sort of persistent and kind preparation, can advance rapidly and recall what they have learned.

Physically mature canines, after a vet check to decide their adequacy, show up prepared to walk and climbing colleagues or on the other hand, assuming they're the right variety and in great condition, running partners.

The early socialization period for grown-up canines is before. This can be uplifting news or terrible news, in light of the fact that either the canine was associated as a doggy… or it wasn't. Expect that what you see is the thing you are continuously going to see. Try not to hope to change a canine who fears your kids into a canine who loves them. On the off chance that you have kids or will associate with them a ton, search for an accommodating canine who effectively searches them out, who answers them with clear interest and warmth and a sweet nature.

Similarly, don't accept that a canine who doesn't seem to like different canines will choose to like the canine you as of now have at home, or your grown-up girl's canine that she brings to the house at whatever point she comes over. Assuming that a canine has no known history with felines, don't take on it assuming you have felines. Many canines are savage toward more modest, quick creatures, and a canine with no feline experience-or who could have pursued or even killed felines in its past life
- can't be anticipated to be a protected family ally for your feline. Search professionally serenely in an encourage home or its unique home together canine with cats.

Can a grown-up canine really bond with another proprietor? The response is totally yes. A portion of the canines generally firmly attached to their proprietors - police K9 corps, drug-sniffing canines, guide canines for the visually impaired, wheelchair help canines, and a lot additional functioning canines don't meet their human accomplices until they are grown-up canines. A few grown-up pet canines will bond with their new proprietors right away. Others will be excessively mistaken or stressed for moment holding, however will rapidly answer another home with kind and fair guidelines, reliable way of behaving from the people, a schedule the canine can come to trust, and bond-upgrading exercises like playing, preparing, strolling and investigating together.

As a matter of fact, a superior inquiry may be "would a youthful little dog be able to genuinely bond with its new proprietor?" An extremely youthful human child will allow anybody to warm and adoring stone it, feed it, and hold it, until abruptly, it arrives at an age where it

realizes who its family is and becomes attentive, for some time, of any other person. Doggies younger than 16-18 weeks are comparative. They can move from one individual to another and climate to climate with little if any pressure or concern. It is the point at which they cross into early pre-adulthood at 16-18 weeks old enough that they start to see a contrast between their relatives and every other person. That is while genuine holding with distinctive individuals starts to occur.

So your fantasy canine may be a grown-up canine rather than a doggy. Grown-up canines can be a lot more straightforward to bring into your life than young doggies. And their potential issues are usually easily solved by having realistic expectations, using common sense, and making sure the adult dog you choose is the right one for you.

15

Good Sources For Adult Dogs

Some of similar hotspots for young doggies can be great hotspots for grown-up canines too. In any case, there are likewise sources that sometimes or never have accessible pups, however quite often have grown-up and juvenile canines available.

Guide Dog or Assistance Dog Organizations

You've presumably seen guide canines and help canines making the rounds with proprietors who need exceptional assistance and backing. What you cannot deny is that many canines who go through preparing to become administration canines like these don't move on from the preparation program effectively. Norms of execution for help canines are very high-and as it should be, taking into account that these canines' future proprietors will rely upon them in a manner not many of us at any point need to rely upon a dog.

Adolescent and youthful grown-up canines who have gone through some or the entirety of their high level preparation yet who won't be put as help canines are classified "profession change" canines. These canines are normally extraordinarily reared Labrador and Golden retrievers or a cross of those two varieties, in addition, periodically, German Shepherds or Standard Poodles. All have been broadly associated by little dog raisers up to around a year old. They have been taken on lifts, into shops and eateries, once in a while even to baseball parks and on trains and planes. They have likewise been educated to answer many signals, and have astounding habits at home and in public.

And not finishing the preparation doesn't imply that these "vocation change" canines are in any capacity severely acted or troublesome. There are many justifications for why a canine probably won't move on from a help canine preparation program, including refusal to defy its overseer in perilous circumstances (an aide canine must be

ready to decline to push ahead into traffic regardless of whether its controller tells it to). These canines are for the most part all around mingled and thoroughly prepared, and make remarkable pets.

Equally extraordinary are resigned administration canines. These are canines who have given long periods of administration as help sidekicks, yet who can never again accomplish the requesting work that this occupation requires. The vast majority of these canines stay with their proprietors/accomplices even after they can never again work, yet some of the time for different reasons that is unimaginable and the canine opens up for reception.

In the event that Labs and Goldens appeal to you, profession change canines and resigned administration canines are an unrivaled wellspring of completely mingled and thoroughly prepared pet canines. There are continuously hanging tight records for them. Contact both public and nearby authorize guide and administration canine associations for details.

Hobby breeders/breed rescues/breed club contacts

Hobby raisers are not only for little dogs! At times these reproducers need to settle on hard decisions about which of their canines to keep and which to make accessible to pet homes. A normal side interest raiser could have two exceptionally encouraging youthful grown-up show prospects however just room in her home to keep one of them. Or then again she could decide to put a resigned top dog whose rearing vocation is over up for reception, so the canine can use whatever remains of his life getting a charge out of "just canine" honors. These canines are not promoted, in light of the fact that the raiser will take however long as important to track down the best home for every one of her canines. If embracing a grown-up canine this way intrigues you, converse with reproducers at canine shows (after they are done appearance in the ring, when have the opportunity to talk). Or then again contact public or neighborhood breed club secretaries to see whether there are accessible grown-up canines in that breed.

Breed salvages are associations given to finding, encouraging, really focusing on, and putting undesirable canines of specific varieties. Pretty much every public variety club has a salvage organizer who monitors accessible canines, their areas and chronicles. There are additionally numerous neighborhood and provincial salvage bunches for specific varieties. The majority of the canines took care of by breed salvage bunches are adults.

Rescue groups and shelters

As noted before, most accessible canines in salvage gatherings and in covers are young people and grown-ups. Numerous teenagers are surrendered for reception in vain more than being typical, undeveloped juvenile canines. As young doggies they were little, charming, and simple to make due, yet as they developed and were not overseen well or prepared, their unique proprietors presently not appreciated living with them. So they were given to a salvage gathering or haven to place.

Fully adult dogs are given up for adoption for reasons ranging from behavioral issues (some serious, such as aggression or severe shyness; some, again, simply stemming from a lack of guidance or training) to death of the owner, to bizarre reasons such as "doesn't match my new carpet" or "rolls on my new sod." Many are strays with obscure chronicles. Keep your "fantasy canine" solidly as a primary concern in the event that you visit an asylum or a salvage gathering, or look through the canines on Petfinder or one more web based posting of accessible salvage dogs.

Veterinarians

Clients regularly contact a confided in veterinarian to assist them with observing homes for canines they can never Once more keep. Again, reasons shift generally. For this situation, as well as talking the proprietor about the canine and, with karma, meeting it in its unique home, you can likewise affirm with the veterinarian that the canine is truly and typically solid and sound. Veterinarians can be a magnificent hotspot for all around adored and really focused on canines whose proprietors should track down new homes for them.

Neighbors, friends, family

It's additionally conceivable, however more uncommon, to take on a canine that a neighbor or companion can't keep. Many individuals, when they observe they can't keep a
darling pet any more, talk first to individuals they know. Assuming you can step in and take the canine yourself, you won't just get a canine you definitely know and like, you'll be a lifeline for your companion, who presently experiences harmony of psyche that their canine will go to a home they trust.

CONCLUSION
What Next?

In this book, you've mastered all that you want to know to find and take on your fantasy canine. You've decided if you're truly prepared, inspected your purposes behind embracing, and realized what doggies resemble and what they need from you. You've investigated a portion of the various characteristics of little dogs and canines that could make them extraordinary pets for you (or not). You've figured out where to track down young doggies and where not to try and look. And you've considered the differences between puppies and adult dogs, in case an adolescent or adult is a better choice for you than a puppy right now. You're ready to invite an astounding little dog or canine into your life.

Before you head out and begin searching for that fantasy canine, I have two last inquiries for you to think about:

What if, after considering all of this, I run across a dog totally different from the one I had in mind and fall in love with it?

Obviously you can alter your perspective assuming you like - it's your fantasy canine, all things considered. But if you have considered yourself and your lifestyle carefully and made some important choices that felt right to you, pause and think hard before applying to adopt a dog who is a very different type from the one you felt would suit you best.

A Rough Collie in full coat can be an amazing canine, radiant looking and good natured, conjuring up dreams of Lassie. But if you decided you did not want to bother with a lot of brushing and grooming, and that you wanted a small-to-medium sized, quiet dog, will you really be happy with a Rough Collie, no matter how beautiful? Unfortunately, Lassie was an actor, with a top professional trainer, and her behavior and adventures on television were fictional. Real collies have real-dog issues such as matting hair, a tendency to bark a lot, and a herding breed's need for regular physical and mental exercise - even when it's muddy outside.

This is the reason it's vital to conclude which canine is your fantasy canine before you
go looking. To those of us who love canines, they are generally magnificent and dear and engaging. But as we've seen in these pages, dogs are very different from each other. Your fantasy canine is the person who is correct for you, who will improve your life and make you can't help thinking about

how you at any point lived without him or her.

What if there is no potential dream dog in the litter or shelter I'm looking at?

Not each litter of doggies contains one that can turn into your fantasy canine. Only one out of every odd salvage or safe house or even side interest raiser will have a little dog or canine that is right for you.

If you are really dedicated to observing your fantasy canine, you won't intentionally bring some unacceptable pup or canine home.

Yes, that could mean leaving an asylum without a canine. It could mean heading out from a salvage's encourage home with basically nothing despite the fact that the restless temporary "mother" sincerely attempted to persuade you that this little dog or canine was ideal for you. It could mean having a genuine discussion with a reproducer you have been working with, clarifying why something about the puppy she believed was ideal for you is raising a warning. For my situation, it has implied flying home alone when the puppy I contracted for most of the way the nation over, seen and endorsed by a companion and associate, was not what I was searching for when I showed up face to face to fly her home under my plane seat. It has likewise implied driving five hours to get a much-needed doggy, going through the night there at a lodging with the little guy, and returning it to the raiser the following morning, driving five hours back to disheartened children.

If you have no faith in yourself to leave despite the fact that it very well may be fundamental, bring an unmistakable looked at and pragmatic disapproved of companion with you when you visit your forthcoming dog(s) or litters of pups. Pay attention to them and trust their judgement.

It's difficult to settle on this decision. But please consider the decision in terms of your lifetime with the dog. Assuming that you track down the solidarity to leave, inside half a month, months, or perhaps a year, you will have found the right canine and

will sink into a blissful and fulfilling canine lifetime with it. In the event that you bring some unacceptable one home, you are setting yourself up for 10 years or a greater amount of pressure and lament. Which is worse, disappointing your children by not bringing home an expected puppy, or having the only dog they will remember throughout their childhoods be vividly different from what you expect and hope for? Which is worse, losing money — even a few hundred dollars — wasting time and energy preparing for a puppy or dog you then choose not to adopt, or spending much, much more in fees to trainers to try to "correct" behaviors you brought home knowingly, even though you did not want them?

Remember, a bashful doggy is probably going to turn into a timid grown-up. An exceptionally pushy doggy is probably going to be trying to deal with. A doggy who has next to zero interest in you as a 7-or 8-week-old is probably not going to turn into the dependable and committed buddy you long for as it ages. These puppies have suitable homes accessible for them, as long as their way of behaving isn't excessively outrageous, yet those are three unique homes. Assuming one suits you, the others don't, and bringing one of those others home since you feel forced to (by a reproducer, a salvage individual, a sanctuary specialist, your youngsters, or your own psyche) isn't helping you or the canine. Recollect that besides the fact that you invest in a potential fifteen years with some unacceptable canine assuming you take this action, *you are similarly sentencing the canine to spending whole lifetime in a house isn't fit to it.*

Evaluating a singular doggy or canine, or a whole litter or gathering of canines, doesn't mean picking the person who most intently approximates what you are searching for. It implies knowing what you are searching for, and not tolerating anything less.

Wait for your fantasy canine. He, or she, is out there, or will be. Select cautiously and carefully, and adhere to your choice once you make it. Both you and the canine will profit from the right choice.

I hope everything works out for you in your Dream Dog search!

What is the ideal age to adopt a puppy?

8-12 weeks is the ideal age range for doggy reception, in most cases.

Younger than about two months is only here and there if at any point smart. More youthful pups are exceptionally juvenile. They are as yet figuring out how to be canines from their mom and littermates. On the off chance that somebody is attempting to persuade you to take a more youthful doggy, it is frequently in light of the fact that by five or a month and a half the puppies are dynamic, need strong food, and are out of nowhere a difficult situation for the individual who is raising them to manage. They are likewise extremely adorable when they are exceptionally youthful. But I suggest looking elsewhere for a puppy if this is the case. The doggy will be a superior grown-up canine assuming it will enjoy its first full seven weeks with its mom and littermates.

There will be times when a younger puppy is already separated from its mother at a younger age, such as when a young litter is brought to a shelter. Assuming you truly do take on a doggy more youthful than about two months old, be ready for an exceptionally juvenile child who needs a lot of rest and rest and incredibly short recesses. You should figure out how to compensate for its deficiency of littermate and mother association time, by observing other youthful viable pups it can have short play periods with, and in a perfect world no less than one more seasoned canine who likes pups for it to collaborate with. You will, obviously, have a more drawn out delay until the more youthful doggy's bladder and entrails are full grown enough for it to endure as the night progressed. Exceptionally youthful doggies are likewise at more serious gamble for sicknesses, so be extremely cautious where you take this puppy.

From 12 to 15 weeks, there isn't a lot of time left in the immeasurably significant socialization window. So know that you should invest additional effort and energy verifying this pup gets appropriately mingled. Likewise, stay away from a doggy this age or more established who shows dreadfulness or an indifference toward individuals. That could never improve.

After about four months, the socialization window has shut. A "pup" north of about four months old enough is actually a youthful juvenile canine. So assuming you are taking a gander at a youthful juvenile canine in this age range, search for one whose reproducer or family who raised it has as of now done a significant part of the associating for you, and one who is well en route to being house trained.

The uplifting news about a youthful young adult is that it will stay asleep from sundown to sunset a whole lot earlier than a 8-week-old doggy, and become house prepared all the more rapidly, assuming that it has been given a decent beginning by its overseers. A somewhat more experienced little guy has a more extended capacity to focus than a child doggy and rushes to learn. This can be a decent age to get a youthful canine if and provided that its requirements, including its socialization needs, have been very much dealt with by whoever raised it through its young puppyhood.

Many side interest reproducers keep more than one pup from a litter to "develop them up" a couple of additional weeks or even months and see who is the better show and rearing possibility between a promising pair. The two little dogs will be similarly very much associated, since the reproducer doesn't know which one she will decide to keep. The other will open up as an extremely pleasant pet. It's likewise conceivable that a family raising a litter, particularly a family with kind and cautious kids, could stand out enough to be noticed to their little dogs that getting a marginally more established puppy from them will work out fine.

However, assuming such a doggy spent the period from birth until about four months or later just with its littermates and absent a lot of human socialization, you might observe that new encounters are exceptionally trying for this pup. The additional time in its litter could have hardened its situation as extremely pushy or exceptionally bashful, and that might be its default position with different canines forever. But even the older pup who bullies its littermates may be fearful with humans if it has had little contact with them, or may freeze with fear in new situations. As I would like to think, just an exceptionally experienced canine proprietor ought to embrace the test of taking on an under-mingled more seasoned puppy.

Some raisers decide not to make their pups accessible until 12 weeks or even four months. Many toy reproducers settle on this decision in light of the fact that their young pups are so tiny and delicate. It merits recollecting that the socialization window is no different for small little dogs concerning medium-sized and huge ones. Ensure you figure out how much socialization the reproducer took on. Did the raiser get her little dogs making the rounds so they could adapt to the world? Did she isolate them from one another for more often than not after they turned two months old enough, so they have figured out how to rest alone, engage themselves with bite toys, and be for the most part autonomous of their littermates and mom? Does the reproducer have them well as they would prefer to being house prepared? In the event that not, search somewhere else for a puppy.

We would like to get littermate puppies to keep each other company (or one for each child). Is that a good idea?

Acquiring littermate young doggies is dangerous. Littermates, similar to human kin, start creating associations with one another from the get-go throughout everyday life. On the off chance that one of the littermates you take on has become pushy with the other, and the subsequent little guy commonly yields to its more decisive sibling or sister, those characteristics will just strengthen as the puppies stay together and become older. Neither one of the wills get the opportunity to adjust its character, so the pushier little guy can figure out how to unwind and the calmer one to advocate for herself a piece more.

Another worry is that the young doggies have known one another for their entire lives and are just now meeting you. It isn't unprecedented for littermates to remain more centered around one another than they are on their proprietors. Specifically, the less decisive of a couple will more often than not hope to its bolder sister or sibling for heading rather than to its proprietor. Obviously there are exemptions, littermate sets who in all actuality do fine for their entire lives together. Nonetheless, embracing littermates isn't suggested in view of the dangers laid out above.

Adopting two random young doggies is a superior wagered. They have no relationship-from-childhood with one another, along these lines they are bound to work out a sound grown-up relationship with one another and with their proprietors. But take care: if one puppy is challenging to raise, two more than doubles the difficulty. Taking two little dogs out for socialization, independently so they don't figure out how to be over-reliant upon one another openly, is more than a great many people will do. Regular day to day division at home is crucial, as well, so they figure out how to be autonomous and furthermore so each fosters an individual relationship with you. Two doggies to take care of, to purchase containers and hardware for, to play with and train… is a ton to manage. Alongside the ideal vision of two adorable young doggies playing together, be certain you imagine one doggy crapping on the floor and the other going through it before you find the opportunity to tidy it up. It will happen.

A greatly improved thought is to raise one doggy to be a wonderful, polite and loving more established juvenile or youthful grown-up canine, who can then be a good example briefly puppy that you bring back a little while later.

Is it better to get a mixed breed or a purebred dog?

If canines ran free in huge gatherings, as they used to in the US before the 1970s despite everything do in many areas of the planet, there would be a solid benefit to taking on a blended variety. The quickest and most grounded, truly fittest and sharpest male was the one to catch and raise with the female, creating ages of shrewd, fit little guys. In any case, a vanishingly modest number of blended breed canines in the US are delivered that way in the 21st century.

Some blended varieties are the results of purposeful breedings between two thoroughbred canines: labradoodles (Labrador retriever x poodle), goldendoodles (Golden retriever x poodle), puggles (pug x beagle), and cockapoos (cocker spaniel x poodle) are a few models. Incidental blended breedings will quite often be between adjoining canines, since not very many canines are permitted to wander loose.

Because of the incredible outcome of the American fix/fix development, most pet canines can't raise. So when an intriguing flawless male canine runs over a similarly interesting physically accessible female and they breed, it's hard to tell how their young doggies will end up. The guardians may be typically and truly solid, however they could not. The little guys will acquire their folks' qualities and will be unequivocally affected by their mom's demeanor. If that temperament is shy or aggressive, and those genes include a tendency toward a condition such as hip dysplasia or Von Willebrands disease, some of those pups will almost certainly have those issues.

Purebreds are intentionally reared, which can be either positive or negative. Little dog factories breed any thoroughbreds they have, no matter what their qualities or their personalities, only for benefit and as frequently as could really be expected. They may likewise intentionally or incidentally produce blended breeds and deal them as "fashioner breeds" with names like schnauzerpoos and cavachons, with excessive cost labels. Like all pup plant little dogs, puppies from these breedings have a

remote possibility of being typically and truly healthy.

Hobby raisers, then again, breed to create the best-quality canines that they would be able. Some utilization complex PC projects to endeavor to keep their canines' hereditary wellbeing as solid as could really be expected, and all furnish their mom canines and little dogs with the best consideration accessible. These pups have a decent possibility being typically and genuinely solid. Nonetheless, the genetic supply of each "unadulterated variety" is, by definition, restricted to different canines of that equivalent variety. Any German Shepherd is hereditarily considerably more like each and every German Shepherd than it is to any Dalmatian. Assuming a physical or conduct condition shows up habitually in that restricted genetic stock, it can spread to different canines of that equivalent variety. Persistent reproducers screen for normal wellbeing and sufficiency issues in their varieties, and do their absolute best not to raise people with these issues. But the limitations of a closed gene pool make it impossible to remove such problems completely.

So there isn't exactly an unmistakable benefit among thoroughbred and blended breed canines. Assuming you can track down a pup from typically and actually sound and solid guardians with great demeanors that has been treasured from birth and painstakingly raised, whether it is a blended variety or a thoroughbred, it has a brilliant possibility turning into a fine pet.

Does a male or a female dog make a better pet?

Some varieties (not all) have personality contrasts among guys and females. Assuming you are taking a gander at a thoroughbred, inquire as to whether there are contrasts in that specific variety. A few varieties have size contrasts between grown-up guys and females, also.

Generally speaking, however, individual disposition matters considerably more than a doggy's sex. There are some sweet-natured and cuddly male canines, and numerous autonomous and emphatic female canines. The converse is likewise evident. Except if you should, for some explanation, don't restrict yourself by choosing ahead of time that you just need a doggy of one specific sex. You could miss the genuine dream little dog in the litter.

What if I want my new puppy to become a therapy dog?

Choose the singular canine for this sort of work with considerably more prominent consideration than you'd utilize choosing a pet, in a perfect world with the direction of a treatment canine expert. Many canines, even in exceptionally "agreeable" breeds, don't have any desire to welcome outsiders at a nursing home or be taken care of by kids they don't know at schools. Be certain you're not extending your own craving to accomplish treatment work onto an apathetic canine. Just canines who really love the work ought to perform therapy.

This book has a companion website, www.dreamdogcentral.com. It includes
a pup blog, stories and tips, reports on the data in this book, and considerably

more. Come visit!

These are what I view as the absolute best assets at the hour of this writing.

Resources on Dog Breeds and Types

It isn't not difficult to track down fair-minded data about various sorts of canines. Individuals who breed or own one sort regularly think it is the absolute best that there is, and may disregard characteristics that could introduce issues for some owners.

My beloved book about canine varieties is The Atlas of Dog Breeds of the World, by Bonnie Wilcox and Chris Walkowicz. It is a gigantic volume with heaps of pictures and portrayals of many canine varieties from around the world. Simply be cautious you don't get your heart set on one that is intriguing even in its local country, which might be extremely distant from yours! There are different books that cover many varieties. It's smart to glance through a few, and see what the depictions share practically speaking, and where they differ.

Online, some variety club sites have gleaming portrayals of their varieties that might disregard or overlook what it's truly similar to reside with one. Different locales are incredible. Be careful with any depictions that sound unrealistic; they more likely than not are. Search for adjusted portrayals that rundown both the delights and the difficulties of living with a specific variety or sort of canine. The best locales for that will more often than not be destinations run by breed salvage associations. They need each canine they spot to remain in its new home, so they are normally exceptionally clear about what you can anticipate. Assuming you have explicit inquiries regarding a variety that its salvage site doesn't reply, email them and ask.

Books About Raising Puppies

Life Skills for Puppies by Helen Zulch and Daniel Mills

Puppy Savvy by Barbara Shumannfang
The Puppy Whisperer by Paul Owens

Puppy Primer, by BrenDa Scidmore and Patricia McConnell Ph. D

Taking Care Of Puppy Business by Gail Pivar and Leslie Nelson

Book for Grown-Ups About Dogs and Kids

Happy Kids, Happy Dogs by Barbara Shumannfang

Book for Children About Raising and Training Puppies

Puppy Training for Kids: Teaching Children the Responsibilities and Joys of Puppy Care, Training, and Companionship, by Colleen Pelar and Amber Johnson

Books About Adopting an Adult Dog

Love Has No Age Limit: Welcoming an ADopted Dog into Your Home, by Patricia McConnell Ph. D and Karen B. London Ph. D

Successful Dog Adoptions, by Sue Sternberg

Book About Housetraining for Puppies and Adult Dogs

Way to Go! Instructions to Housetrain a Dog of Any Age, by Karen B. London Ph.D. what's more, Patricia B. McConnell Ph.D

Books About Training, for Adult Dogs (and Puppies Too!)

Dog-Friendly Dog Training, by Andrea Arden

Family FrienDly Dog Training: A Six Week Program for Yourself as well as Your Dog, by Patricia B McConnell Ph.D. what's more, Aimee M Moore

Informative Books About the Human-Dog Bond:

The Other EnD of the Leash, by Patricia McConnell Ph. D

Bones Would Rain From the Sky, by Suzanne Clothier

Book About Puppy Stages and Development

Another Piece of the Puzzle: Puppy Development, by Pat Hastings and Erin Ann Rouse

Book About Evaluating The Structure of A Dog Who You Would Like to Live An Active Lifestyle

Structure in real life: The Makings of a Durable Dog, by Pat Hastings and Wendy E Wallace DVM cVA

DVD About Evaluating The Structure of Puppies

Puppy Puzzle - Evaluating Structural Quality, by Pat Hastings

Recommended YouTube channels

Puppy and Dog Training and Behavior

Kikopup

Thefamilydog

Facebook group, wonderful for guiding you as you socialize your puppy

The Social Puppy Games 2.0

ACKNOWLEDGEMENTS

I need to thank the group at The Master Wordsmith for their direction and all their work for my sake, without which making this book would have been truly challenging in the event that certainly feasible. James Ranson, Tyler Wagner, Meg Sylvia, and Joe Brachocki, numerous thanks.

Working on the photographs for this book with Lynn Terry of Lynn Terry Photography was a genuine delight. Much appreciated Lynn; I can hardly wait to work with you again.

Thanks to companions and associates who read the composition at various stages and offered supportive and wise remarks that very superior the last form: Kama Brown, Cinder Wilkinson-Kenner, Dr. Celeste Walsen, Shane Whelan, Paul Lehmann, Lucy Bailey, and Tracy Buck, bless your heart. And many thanks to "beta testers" Michael and Kerry Whelan, who used an early draft of this book as a guide while making decisions about a puppy adoption and gave me invaluable practical feedback. The way that they found the book supportive and are exceptionally content with the pup they picked was most encouraging.

Finally, because of canine master specialist Kay Laurence and my kindred understudies in her Intelligent Dog Trainer Course. My contemplations about and perspectives toward the organization among canines and their kin have perpetually been improved -, I trust - by what I have gained from you. And to Dr. Jesús Rosales-Ruiz, ever steady of my learning and my tasks.

Printed in Great Britain
by Amazon

15065512R00046